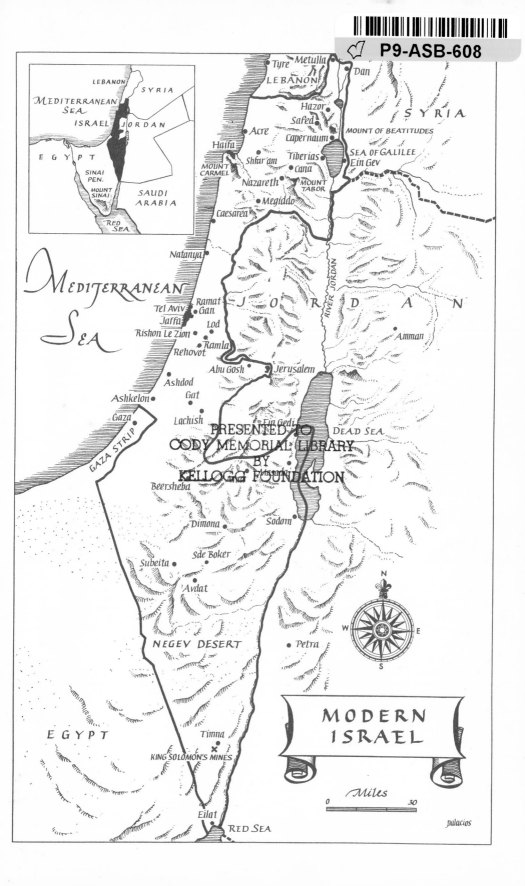

MODERN
ISRAEL

Miles

0   30

palacios

Also by Oden Meeker

THE LITTLE WORLD OF LAOS

WORLD BACKGROUND BOOKS

AFGHANISTAN by Christine Weston
CEYLON by Christine Weston
GREECE by Helen Hill Miller
ISRAEL REBORN by Oden Meeker
THE NEW AFRICA by Ellen and Attilio Gatti
MEDITERRANEAN SPOTLIGHTS by Attilio Gatti
HERE IS ALASKA (*Revised Edition*) by Evelyn Stefansson
HERE IS THE FAR NORTH by Evelyn Stefansson

Israel Reborn

A WORLD BACKGROUND BOOK

Illustrated with photographs and maps

Israel Reborn

by ODEN MEEKER

CHARLES SCRIBNER'S SONS NEW YORK

ACKNOWLEDGMENTS

Grateful acknowledgment is made for permission to use the following:

Photographs on pages 20–21, 22, 23, 24–25, 28, 29, 30, 31 (bottom), 33, 49, 53, 54, 67, 68, 69, 72–73, 75, 77, 78, 80–81, 86, 106, 110, 112, 118, 127, 128, 130–131, 141, 144, 145, 147, 149, 150, 152, 158, 159, 161, 162–163, 167, 175 from the Israel Government Press Office.

Photographs on pages 31 (top), 32, 35, 36, 41, 52, 61, 62–63, 64, 95, 96, 102, 104, 114, 122, 123, 132, 133, 135, 137, 139, 156–157 from the Zionist Archives and Library.

Photographs on pages 18, 38–39, 50, 59, 66, 84, 88, 91, 154, 173 from the Israel Information Services.

Photographs on pages 43, 70, 146 from the Israel Government Tourist Office.

Photographs on pages 124, 170 by Hans H. Pinn.

Photographs on pages 56 by Willem Van De Poll, 134 by Fritz Henle, 143 from the Monkmeyer Press Photo Service.

Maps on pages 92, 116 by Rafael Palacios.

For Bertie, with love

CONTENTS

LIST OF ILLUSTRATIONS

Chapter 1

A NEW NATION
FROM AN ANCIENT PEOPLE

On a map showing the web of airlines connecting the great cities of the world, the State of Israel is so small it is difficult to find. Sometimes it is reduced to a circle marking the airport, with the name of the largest city, Tel Aviv, standing bravely out in the Mediterranean. On a map of the Eastern Hemisphere in my almanac, Israel has disappeared completely.

The map does not really matter. Israel is very much a part of the world. Here, on a bit of land at the southeastern end of the Mediterranean, an extraordinary people have made an ancient dream come true.

This is the land called Canaan, the Promised Land, Israel and Judah in the Bible; then Palestine and the Holy Land. It has known many masters, first the Canaanites and then the Israelites, and has been harried by the Moabites, Midianites, Ammonites and the Philistines. It was conquered by the ancient Babylonians, Greeks, Egyptians and Syrians, and governed for seven centuries by the Romans. It was invaded and occupied by the Arabs in the seventh century, the Crusaders in the eleventh century, the Tartars in the thirteenth century and the Turks in the seventeenth century. As Palestine, the land that is now Israel and parts of Jordan and Egypt was administered as a League of Nations mandate by Britain between the end of the

Aerial view of Dizengoff Circle, Tel Aviv

First World War and 1948. But for thousands of years, even during their exile, this has been the homeland of the Jewish people.

From the air in the evening as the big planes come in from Italy and Greece, the Promised Land is a scattering of lights along the shore. It is only on the ground and in the airport that the quality of the country begins to strike the traveler. In the lines moving toward the immigration officers are Americans and Canadians and South Africans—visitors from the Jewish communities in other countries, businessmen and people who just want to see for themselves how the new state is faring. There are pale Eastern European Jews in long black coats, beards and wide-brimmed hats; swarthy, French-speaking Jews from North Africa; and hearty tourists so festooned with cameras and equipment that they seem to have been studying their part. There are Latin Americans at the airport, and Scandinavians and Indians and Turks and Greeks, single visitors and delegations, Burmese and African students, Nigerians with their boldly patterned robes and embroidered

18

pillbox hats. The crowd is a measure of the interest and curiosity this new state has aroused. On the other side of the customs barrier are the Israelis and their country.

My wife Bertie and I asked on entering Israel, as we had been advised, that our visas be stamped on the foreign currency exchange card we were issued. The immigration officer was alert, both polite and sure of himself, burned brown-black and wearing a neat military mustache, a dark blue visored cap and short-sleeved suntans. He asked us why, and we explained that it was to avoid the difficulty of having to apply for new passports unmarked with Hebrew if we ever wanted to travel through any of the Arab states in the future. He accepted this and simply stamped our cards, handing them back to us with our passports.

We took them with mixed emotions, feeling it was rather tacky of us to ask the people here to make concessions to the prejudices of others against them. Then, as we left, we noticed something we had sometimes seen on hot summer days in the subway in New York: the blue serial number of a Nazi concentration camp tattooed on the man's forearm.

The State of Israel is not a large place. Where my wife and I lived—just north of Tel Aviv—it is less than ten miles from the sea to the Jordanian border, and nowhere is the country more than sixty-five miles wide. Yet in it live two and a half million people, about half of them settlers who have come to the country since independence in 1948. Most of them—before they became Israelis—were refugees, fleeing the Nazi terror in Europe and persecution of many kinds in many different countries. If the United States gave shelter to over a hundred million refugees in the next ten years, this would be equivalent to the ingathering of Jews in Israel so far.

At the birth of the State of Israel, following a 1947 United Nations recommendation that Palestine be partitioned into

Rosh Zohar in the Negev

Jewish and Arab states, the new nation was invaded by five Arab neighbors, countries bitterly opposed to the re-creation of a Jewish homeland, and openly bent on the extermination of the six hundred and fifty thousand Jews already there.

Somehow, the new Israelis stood their ground and managed to secure eight thousand square miles, an area slightly larger than New Jersey. From the brief border with Lebanon and Syria on the north, the land now called Israel follows the Mediterranean coast for a hundred and seventeen miles. Jordan lies to the east, and Egypt to the south and west, with a corner of Saudi Arabia almost touching Israel's southern tip. About halfway down, the land widens abruptly to form a long triangle which tapers to a point at Eilat, a port on the Gulf of Aqaba which leads to the Red Sea and the Indian Ocean.

The triangle is Israel's Negev desert, just over half the area of

the country. But the desert, for centuries the preserve of the nomadic Bedouin, was in Biblical times a partly-cultivated desert within the flourishing Fertile Crescent of the ancient world. Now, sections of pipe large enough for a man to stand in are being laid from Lake Tiberias in the north down to the Negev, bringing water to make the desert bloom again.

Half of the new immigrants to the country are settled in the Negev—shopkeepers, professional men, politicians and scholars who become pioneers in the cooperative settlements of their new country. If reclamation of the Negev is successful, Israel should be able to support a population of four to five million.

Water is the key. New methods of turning salt water into fresh are being tried, as is the use of solar energy for heat and power. The lessons learned by the Israelis in the Negev could be of great value throughout the Middle East and North Africa,

Yetvata, a pioneering kibbutz in the Negev

and in countries like Australia and Chile and even parts of the United States—wherever there is the challenge of development of arid lands.

People come from around the world to see what is happening in the Negev, to visit the cooperative rural settlements called moshavim and the communal ones called kibbutzim, to learn something from the wide range of social experiments within a democratic framework. Burmese come to study how to go about farming in frontier regions subject to attack, a problem they face in their own country. Burmese girls (Christian, Moslem and Buddhist) have come for courses with the Israeli army. Women are conscripted in Israel and girls in their late teens,

22

sunburned and in uniform, are a part of the Israeli landscape. Social workers from many countries come to study the integration into a new society of vast numbers of refugees and immigrants—a familiar problem in London, Paris and New York.

Israel has been called the most successful of all the underdeveloped countries, and it is not surprising. She has launched meteorological rockets and is exploring peaceful uses of atomic energy. Israel has almost no natural resources, but she has built up a thriving export trade in citrus and runs successful international shipping and air lines, determinedly going after the overseas markets for everything from phosphates to fashion. A good portion of the world's diamond-cutting trade has been brought to Israel. As a source of income, tourism is the second harvester of foreign exchange.

The visitors find themselves in a paradoxical place, a country that blends the old with the new, the modern with the picturesque. In Israel, it is a time of helicopter tours, of eleven-month courses turning young immigrants into electricians and welders; yet a time when Bible quizzes are a national sport,

A new kibbutz member drinks water Arab fashion

and road signs point the way to Nazareth and Jerusalem. The tempo of the country is brisk, sometimes driving. Life is casual and informal. Manual labor is highly paid, sometimes better so than the professions. There is a surplus of doctors. The lively arts are lively: music, theater, literature and graphics are all in robust health.

Life in Israel is saturated with its Biblical past. For this truly is the Holy Land: Jerusalem is the most sacred of cities to Jews and Christians, and one of the holiest to Moslems. What we know as Western civilization is descended from that of the Greeks, the Romans and the Hebrews; and the Judeo-Christian culture of Israel, its religion and its law, are a part of our daily lives in a thousand different ways that we seldom recognize. The land of Israel, between the mountains and the sea, has been the bridge between Asia and Africa and Europe since man's earliest wanderings.

So they press forward, these astonishing people, the new Israelis. Each month a few thousand more come, many of them refugees with little more than the clothes on their backs. One grave problem still faces them and all their neighbors. During the War of Independence, more than six hundred thousand Arabs fled their homes in what is now Israel, planning to return when the war was over and, they were promised, the Jews driven into the sea. Many thousands have been accepted back by the Israeli government in an effort to reunite families. But the rest—their number now grown to one million two hundred thousand according to United Nations estimates—wait just across the frontier, mostly in Jordan, and in the Gaza Strip administered by Egypt. The Arab states consider themselves still at war with Israel. Watchtowers still stand on Israeli farms.

A girl stands guard on a haystack in Kibbutz Amazia

The deadlock has continued for more than a decade. Meanwhile, the rivers of the Jordan Valley cry for mutual development by Israel and Jordan. The end of hostilities (there is now only an armistice), the agreement at least to live and let live, resettlement of the refugees, and a joint effort to use mutual resources are all seen by both the United States and the United Nations as vital to the prosperity of the region. And Israel, too, is on record as recognizing that the only solution is some sort of peace between the neighbors.

Chapter 2

THE JEWS

Ninety per cent of the population of Israel is Jewish, and of such variety that this majority at times seems like an aggregation of minorities. The remaining ten per cent of the population is Arab, mainly Moslem and Christian, with some Druzes and a scattering of others.

Only about a third of the Jewish population was born in Israel. These are the sabras, named after the fruit of the cactus which thrives in the desert. The rest are immigrants from more than a hundred different lands. The largest groups are the Ashkenazim from Northern and Eastern Europe, and the Sephardim, descendants of the Spanish and Portuguese Jews, expelled from the Iberian Peninsula the year of Columbus' first voyage to America, and shortly after, who settled wherever they could find refuge. The Sephardim who had established themselves mainly in North Africa and the Middle East, are known in Israel as Oriental Jews. Many Jews never left this region. By now, with heavy immigration from North Africa and the Middle East, most Israeli families, though they may come from neighboring Arab countries, are as much a part of the traditional local scenery as are the Christians or the Moslems.

Others come from nearly every part of the world. There are Jews from Germany and Austria, the Congo and Curaçao, Italy and Egypt. There are over four hundred thousand immigrants from Poland. In the first few weeks after our arrival, we met Israelis born in Kurdistan, China, Siberia, Lithuania, Brazil, Ecuador, Dublin and Brooklyn. Nearly every ship and plane brings more immigrants. In the streets there used to be trucks full of suitcases, and waiting for the port customs officers, lines of quiet bearded men with broad hats; pale small boys with black skullcaps and the traditional ringlets in front of their ears; and women with simple long dresses and kerchiefs over their heads. Now, there are increasing numbers from North Africa, some of the older men in Arab dress. From wherever they come, most of them are poor.

The immigrants bring with them many different cultures, different tongues, different dress, different music and different food. Kol Israel, the Voice of Israel, broadcasts to Israeli listeners every day in a dozen languages, including Ladino which is based on medieval Spanish and is still spoken by the Sephardim. The Israeli staff of five in CARE's Tel Aviv office

Orthodox Chassidic boy with traditional earlocks called "Payot"

A Yemenite woman

where I worked spoke nine languages fluently, and could manage in four more. The English in town ranges from Oxonian to Australian, from Cockney to the Bronx.

There are marked differences between the founding fathers and the later pioneers; between the immigrants from Czarist Russia and the later refugees from Germany; between all the Europeans and the Jews from North Africa and the Middle East. The gulf is wide that separates the cosmopolitan Viennese from the Yemenites who for the past twenty-five hundred years have lived isolated in the far southwestern tip of the Arabian Peninsula. Yet there are things they share, strong bonds which bind together the most scattered of the Jews returned to Israel after their long exile.

29

A Morroccan woman in the Beersheba market place

First, there is the legacy of persecution and discrimination in so many countries over so many years, a sort of brotherhood of suffering. If an individual has escaped humiliation and persecution, then his family or friends will have suffered. All, as Jews, are acutely aware of the six million who perished in Europe in our time just because of their Jewish origin. This they call the Holocaust, the most terrible ordeal the Jewish people has survived.

30

In all the centuries since Rome conquered Israel, the Jews have lived in scattered minorities under alien rule. It has been a time of persecution, now moderate, now almost non-existent, but often savage. This memory is shared by Jewry throughout the world. In countries like the United States or Canada or Britain, it is difficult perhaps to understand the apprehension, fear and desperation of Jews in other countries, the need of a homeland where Jews from anywhere in the world could find refuge. Israel has become that place, and as immigration continues every year, every day, the new Israelis are deeply conscious of this fact.

An immigrant from Persia

An immigrant from North Africa

Religion is the greatest of the cohesive forces that have kept the Jews distinct as a people all these stormy years, and it unites the surviving fragments brought together again in Israel. Through the generations of officially instigated persecution in Russia and Poland, when their faith brought them only abuse and humiliation, extortion backed by law and even the loss of their lives in the pogroms that wracked Eastern Europe, Russian and Polish Jews kept their faith. In Yemen, cut off from the rest of the world, relegated to perpetually inferior status and with their children often forcibly converted to Islam, somehow they kept their faith.

A Youth Aliya boy at prayer

A group of Rabbis reading the Torah during the Hakhel ceremony in Jerusalem

Bucharians dance with the Torah

In modern Israel, the Old Testament and the millennia of Jewish history are very much a part of everyday life for everyone from the ultra-Orthodox to the non-believer. It is possible for an Israeli to say, "I am not religious," but it is impossible not to be affected in a thousand ways every day by Biblical law and religion and the way of life which has been built on them.

Only food which is kosher, that is which conforms to traditional dietary laws, is served by the national air and steamship lines, hotels and most restaurants. Following the complex set of injunctions in the Old Testament, pork and shellfish are forbidden (a rule which probably originated as a highly sensible health precaution), and meat must not be served with milk, butter or other dairy products. Even in the non-kosher restaurants, a steak seldom tastes to the visitor like a steak, for it has been bled until its flavor is ghostly. Because of the Biblical prohibition against work on the Sabbath, almost all public transport in Israel—trains, buses (except in Haifa) and the Israeli inland and overseas airlines—comes to a halt at sundown Friday and does not begin to roll again until sundown

33

Saturday. Taxis, being private, (and the Israelis, being individualists) continue to run. There is no mail on the Sabbath, there are no newspapers, and no movies or theatres are open. Throughout Israel the Sabbath prevails.

The names of the Israelis and the names of their towns and villages and streets, are the names of the Bible, ancient, not remote, and very much alive. There is Jerusalem and Nazareth and Galilee, and Rachel Street and King David Street and King Saul Boulevard. Ruth, Sarah, Miriam and Esther are popular first names, and so are Abraham, Isaac, Aaron, Samuel, Nahum and Israel. It is not unusual to meet infants named after Solomon or Moses.

The morning paper gives better-than-Olympic coverage to the quadrennial Jewish games called the Maccabiah, after the Maccabees who, during the greater part of the century and a half before Christ, ruled the last independent Kingdom of Israel. Archeological discoveries rival sport; the finding of the scrolls of Bar Kochba, the leader of Israel's last, desperate rebellion against Rome in 132 A.D., was given greatest prominence and treated as a mixture of high adventure and an affair of state.

The marriage contracts of today follow the same Biblical law as those of Bar Kochba's time, which were written on tightly-rolled papyri and found in the Cave of Letters in the Negev. Moslem, Christian and Jewish marriages are performed in mosque, church and synagogue. There is no provision for marriage between faiths; the nearest accessible place couples can go for a civil marriage is Cyprus.

Simon Bar Kochba in his struggle for freedom emphasized things Hebrew, and in his government encouraged the use of the Hebrew language rather than Aramaic which was the language spoken by Christ, and then the vernacular of the

An Israeli soldier blows the shofar

country. In Israel today, Hebrew again is the language of the army, and again the Bible is the guide. Rabbis serve as chaplains in military synagogues, and on the High Holy Days, during combat, the Rabbinate had to give troops in exposed forward positions special exemption from blowing the shofar, the ram's horn, since it might disclose them.

It is entirely in temper with the place and the times that Israel's prominent Biblical archeologist should be ex-Chief-of-Staff Yigael Yadin, who discovered the Bar Kochba scrolls.

The defense forces and the national language are used to weld together the diverse population. Since nearly everyone between the ages of eighteen and twenty-six spends two and a half years in the armed services (two years for women), and no one leaves the services without a basic education and knowledge of Hebrew, conscription is one of the great unifying factors in the nation, particularly for the new immigrants. And, as always, the basis of education, religion and law, culture, and of the nation itself, is the Old Testament.

35

Zionism—the movement for re-creating a Jewish nation in Israel—was the idea which flickered more brightly during the latter part of the nineteenth century when more and more joined the thousands who had already left Eastern Europe to live with the Jews remaining in the Holy Land, all of them firm in their belief that Israel was their home, a land in which it was good to live, in which they must live, no matter how difficult their daily lives might be. Zionism took fire when a young Austrian journalist named Theodor Herzl covered the Dreyfus trial in Paris in 1894. Herzl was so moved by the anti-Jewish pillorying of the French army captain falsely convicted of treason and sent to Devil's Island, that he spent the rest of his life working for the return to the Jews of the land that had once been their home. An extraordinary figure with pensive eyes and the long black beard of a younger prophet, he was a man of great simplicity and a visionary, magnetic leader. With Herzl, with Chaim Weizmann, the gentle Russo-British chemist and indefatigable worker for his people's cause, and with a number of remarkably capable men and women among their leaders, the Zionists accomplished the nearly impossible. Out

Theodor Herzl

of a people scattered for nearly two thousand years, a people who had no territory, spoke no common language, who lived miserably in some countries and on sufferance in others, the Zionists created a living nation.

The character of the early settlers tells a great deal about that of the independent Israel to come. First to arrive were the Russians who in the latter nineteenth century joined the Palestinian Jews in forming communal agricultural settlements. By 1900, there were twenty such settlements. The return to the soil and working with one's hands became articles of faith, in great part reaction against the stereotype of the Jew as a wan, unhealthy townsman, a merchant or moneylender, a man who refused to work with his hands. The fact that the stereotype grew out of the forcible confining of the Jews in Eastern Europe to ghettoes in the cities and to a few livelihoods like moneylending did not alter the unattractiveness of this picture. Anti-Semitism fed on it. Opposed to it was the life of the simple, clean and hearty son of the soil; a way of life, their detractors implied, spurned by the Jews.

But certainly the Jewish pioneers themselves believed that a hand to the plow and manual labor of all sorts were in themselves good after the artificially restricted life of Jews in Eastern Europe. Clearing the stony land, breaking rocks, struggling to bring water to the desert, draining the malarial swamps, fighting off attacks on the settlements, these were admired as the best things a man or a woman could do. Now, more than eighty years later, a member of a cooperative frontier settlement or a manual laborer still enjoys a prestige in Israel which is hard for the professional man to match.

The early Russian pioneers were joined by Germans and others from Eastern and Central Europe, until by 1914, in the last years of Turkish rule over Palestine, there were eighty-five thousand Jews living in the country. Some were born there, but more came because they were enthusiasts, idealists who dreamed of the new country they would build. In the beginning, the agricultural settlements nearly foundered, but were rescued by the Baron Edmond de Rothschild of France whose generosity made possible not only their survival but success. At the start of the First World War, there were fifty Jewish communities in Palestine, about eighty per cent of which were farming villages. Many of them were collective or cooperative, the forerunners of the contemporary kibbutzim (joint ownership of land, equipment and some housing, and with communal care of children) and of the moshavim (smallholders with cooperative purchase and marketing). These were a social experiment which has attracted a steady stream of interested visitors from other countries.

Now, inevitably, as the country becomes more secure, life in the kibbutzim becomes less glamorous. George Mikes, in his warm and perceptive book, *Milk and Honey*, has written of the pioneers: "The great ideal has been fulfilled—and now they have little to look forward to . . . There is always a great deal of frustration in the fulfillment of dreams."

Many of the new pioneers head for the cities instead of the frontier settlements; children of the kibbutzim and moshavim are drawn to the bright lights, as are country people all over the world. But still, one out of every twenty Israelis is a member of a kibbutz. About sixty per cent of the new immigrants become pioneers in the desert or the sparsely settled north of the country, and the collective and cooperative communities continue to play a vital role in the settling and the guarding of the Israeli frontier.

Kibbutz Ayelet Hashahar in Upper Galilee

After publication in 1917 of the British government's *Balfour Declaration*, which favored the establishment of a national home in Palestine for the Jewish people, the League of Nations entrusted this ex-Turkish territory to Britain under mandate, with express instructions to "facilitate Jewish immigration" and to encourage "close settlement on the land." The old longing "to go and die in Jerusalem" had become translated into enthusiasm to go to Palestine and there build the new Zion. In spite of violence from Arabs opposed to both Jewish immigration and their purchase of land and settlement, and in spite of later severe restrictions on these by a British government unable to reconcile conflicting commitments to Jew and Arab, more and more Jewish immigrants made their way to Israel, both legally and illegally. During and after the Second World War their numbers were swelled by many who had managed to escape annihilation by the Nazis. Forced to emigrate from Iraq, declared stateless persons in Egypt, harried by the governments of the Arab states without exception, the once thriving Jewish communities of North Africa and the Middle East found themselves defenseless and under attack. Many of their members came to Israel.

All but two thousand of the thirty-two thousand Jews in Libya came to Israel. An airlift brought a hundred thousand from Iraq within twelve months. Most remarkable of all was Operation Magic Carpet which brought almost all the remaining forty-five thousand of the Jewish colony in Yemen back to Israel after an exile of 2,577 years.

In the 1880's, the Yemenites had begun to move to Palestine. Then, following the Palestine Arab riots of 1929, the Imam Yahya of Yemen forbade further emigration. Some Yemenite Jews managed to get as far as the neighboring British protectorate of Aden, where they lived, destitute, until permitted to enter Palestine four years later.

Yemenite Jews waiting to be flown to Israel

After the United Nation's decision in 1947 to partition
Palestine into Arab and Jewish states, there were serious riots
in Aden, numbers of Jews were killed, and the Jewish quarter
was burned. The old Imam was murdered in Yemen the following year, and in the anarchy that followed, the Jews were looted
by troops of both the Imam's sons, fighting each other for the

41

throne. Finally, the British agreed to the departure of Yemenite Jews from Aden, the Sultans who controlled the way between Yemen and Aden gave their permission, and the Yemeni authorities agreed to let their Jewish people go. But Egypt barred the Suez Canal, and, at that time, the Gulf of Aqaba as well.

Following Jewish Agency couriers through the unmarked desert, forty-five thousand men, women and children made the trek, most of them on foot, with little more to their names than the Scrolls of the Law from their synagogues. They were without food or medicine or doctors. Malaria was raging, and many of the refugees fell sick. But they got to Aden and were carried to Israel, they said, "on the wings of eagles"—a flight of old American planes which ferried back and forth until all forty-five thousand were safe.

There are now over a hundred thousand Yemenites in Israel, a skillful and industrious people who are jewelry workers, artisans, small traders, farmers and manual laborers. They are slight, swarthy and attached to their own customs. They possess a great store of folk songs and folk dances and enough political awareness to send their own man to the legislature to represent their interests. After the years of isolation and persecution, the Yemenites are an asset and a source of strength to Israel.

In a report called *The Jewish Exodus from the Arab Countries and the Arab Refugees*, the Israel Ministry for Foreign Affairs has summed up eloquently the return of the Yemenites from exile:

"That was the end of yet another great Jewish community in the Arab world whose origins went back to the days of the Bible." [It quotes an Israeli observer:] " 'In spite of all the difficulties encountered, it was a very different liquidation than that in the countries under Nazi control. No graves were dug, no doxology was sung. A whole living community with their Holy Books was saved from peril and degradation . . .' "

A Yemenite silversmith

The escape of the Yemenites in the great metal birds was one of a thousand ways the exiles returned to Israel. Fewer than four in a hundred could pay for their passage; most were stripped of their belongings as they left the countries in which they were born. Somehow, with the help of Jews around the world, Israel gathered them in. The Jewish population of six hundred and fifty thousand at the time of Israel's independence was more than doubled by the end of 1951. There were more than a million immigrants by 1961, a staggering and unprecedented burden for any country to assume, let alone a fledgling state which had just declared its own independence and was fighting for its life against the invading forces of its neighbors.

The response of Israel and Zionists around the world was heroic. Jewish refugees were gathered from the displaced persons' camps in Europe and made the journey, often hazardous, to points of embarkation in Italy or France, where they sailed on the hulks hastily collected by Israel as her merchant marine.

The refugees—or newcomers, as Israel prefers to call them—arrived in the middle of the war, disembarking while Tel Aviv was bombed and Jerusalem cut off. They were under siege by an enemy sworn to exterminate them.

There came veterans of the European underground and the resistance movements, survivors of the concentration camps, seven thousand of the eleven thousand Jews left in Yugoslavia, most of the Jews from Czechoslovakia and Bulgaria, nearly half of those in Turkey, five thousand from China, over a hundred thousand from Rumania, and a few from the Soviet Union. A remnant of the Bagdad Jews came from Bombay, and a thousand Cochin Jews from India's Malabar Coast to the south.

The thousands of refugees crowded on the decks of the immigrant ships found waiting for them a new government and a people willing to share what little they had. The armed forces enlisted volunteers from many countries. Housing, medical care and public health measures were all improvised from next to nothing for the newcomers. Accepting all Jewish immigrants without question meant taking care of an unusually high proportion of the elderly and ill, people who were physically and mentally disabled, children without relatives— and all this in the midst of a desperate struggle for survival. It was a brilliant job.

From the tents and shacks of the transient camps called ma'abarot, the immigrants were helped to settle all over Israel. They arrived wearing the babushkas and cloth caps of Eastern Europe, the shapeless scarves and overcoats of refugees the world over, the dark suits of professional men, the bangles and kerchiefs and long robes of the women from the Arab countries. After a few months in the new villages and frontier settlements, a sizeable proportion had changed to simple cotton dresses, shirts and shorts, and the national tembel cap, like a gob's hat with the brim turned down.

Discouraged by the isolation and loneliness of the farms, some of the first settlers drifted back to the cities. More stayed. No one was forced to go and live where he was asked, but the advantages of better housing, better facilities of many sorts offered to settlers in the new villages made them increasingly attractive. Access roads were built, electricity was brought in, and, most helpful, young Israel-born sabras were sent to join the new arrivals, teaching, working in the fields, guarding the settlements along the frontier.

After 1954, when there were still nearly a hundred thousand persons living in the ma'abarot, a determined effort was made to resettle all those still left in these transient camps. Many of the inhabitants were reluctant to go. They preferred to cling to the neighborhoods they knew, to the familiar inconveniences of the camps rather than to cope with the unfamiliar problems of a new home in a new place. Others made their own way. In the modest, middle-class neighborhood of small gardens and smaller houses in which we live outside Tel Aviv (it is quieter and greener than most places in the city), there is a ma'abara of shacks along the sand dunes between us and the sea. Our neighbors come from Germany, Austria, Russia, Egypt, Morocco and the United States, and many of the less fortunate ones began life in Israel on the dunes or in a similar ma'abara. One friend, who had run textile factories in Yugoslavia and served there as an army officer, first found work in his fifties as a casual laborer, then a job as manager of several dispensaries and clinics, and now shares with his wife and two sons a small stucco bungalow with a tile roof.

It is a dismal commentary on man's ability to make a better world that now, over fifteen years after the Second World War, there are more refugees than there were at the war's end. Slowly, the displaced persons' camps of Europe have emptied, and new homes have been found for the people there. Meanwhile, there have been new waves of refugees from East Germany, India, Pakistan, China and Tibet, from Algeria and half a dozen parts of Africa south of the Sahara. A few million still live in camps, waiting to be resettled.

Only twice in modern times, when the world has seen a sudden large influx of refugees, have homes, new jobs, new places in the sun been found for almost all those cast adrift: in the case of the Hungarian uprising, when countries quickly and generously found room for the two hundred thousand who fled; and in the case of Israel, which has so far found room for a million.

Israel's new immigrants are proving good citizens. In writing about them, their government has, appropriately, used two quotations. One, of course, is from the Bible:

> And they shall come that were lost in the land of Assyria,
> And they that were dispersed in the land of Egypt.
>
> ISAIAH: 27 : 13

The other is a part of the sonnet by Emma Lazarus engraved on a tablet at the Statue of Liberty:

> ... Give me your tired, your poor,
> Your huddled masses yearning to breathe free,
> The wretched refuse of your teeming shore,
> Send these, the homeless, tempest-tossed, to me . . .

Chapter 3

THE ARABS

Ten per cent of Israel's population is mainly Arab. Those of the non-Jewish ten per cent who are not Arab are— like the Jewish ninety per cent—a mosaic of the peoples and religions left by the migrations and invasions, transportations and conversions which this crossroads has known over the past four thousand years. The Canaanites, Moabites, Phoenicians and other ancient nations long have been lost among the general population. One sees no trace of the two waves of Mongol invaders who swept over the land. But there are many other pockets of people left.

Of the group of Armenian refugees who settled in Palestine during and after the First World War, perhaps a thousand remain in Israel (about half of the two million Armenians had been killed by the Turks, the greatest known slaughter of one group of people by another until the killing of the Jews in Europe). There are in Israel villages of Moslem Circassians whose ancestors came from the Russian Caucasus. There are divergent sects like that of the Druzes (twenty-five thousand) whose patron is Jethro, the father-in-law of Moses, and who fought with the Jews against the Arabs; and the members (three hundred) of the Baha'i movement, a universalist faith

48

A Druze leader

with many followers in the United States and England, and with headquarters, a Persian garden and a golden-domed temple, in Haifa. Then there are the Samaritans—like the Good Samaritan in the Bible—a small, separate group of which there are about four hundred left in Israel and which recognizes only the five books of Moses and the Book of Joshua.

Unlike other great cities of the world, Jerusalem, Tel Aviv and Haifa shelter relatively small colonies of foreign sojourners. The thousand African and Asian students in these cities and elsewhere in Israel are not particularly conspicuous. At any one time, there are eight to nine thousand American tourists or residents in the country, but both groups seem well integrated into Israeli life. Then there are the missionaries. There is a wonderful profusion of monks, nuns and priests who look after the holy places and churches: Greek, Roman and Maronite Catholic, Ethiopian and Egyptian Coptic, Armenian and Greek Orthodox. Protestants range from Episcopalians and

49

In front of the Church of the Annunciation in Nazareth

Anglicans to Presbyterians, Lutherans, Baptists, Seventh Day Adventists and Pentecostals. The YMCA and the Quakers have run a number of social service projects. And there is always—as there has been for hundreds of years—a handful of Christians who have come to wait in the Holy Land for the expected second coming of Christ and the end of the world.

Most of the Arab minority in Israel is either Moslem (about one hundred and sixty thousand) or Christian (fifty thousand). Before 1948, there were about three quarters of a million Arabs, giving them a slight majority over the six hundred and fifty thousand Jews then in the country. By the end of 1948, after the invasion and the fighting which followed, over six hundred

50

thousand Arabs fled the country. They left only a hundred and eight thousand Arabs in Israel. Thirty-one thousand Arab refugees soon returned, and another fifty thousand have since been permitted to come back to rejoin their families. Altogether, the Arab population of Israel has grown to two hundred and thirty thousand, while their Jewish fellow citizens number two million.

Meanwhile, according to United Nations estimates, the number of Arab refugees and their children outside Israel has doubled (an exact census has never been permitted by the governments of the countries in which they now find themselves). Known as Palestinian refugees, most have lived since 1948 in the refugee camps in Jordan and in the Gaza Strip administered by Egypt. About twenty per cent—mainly skilled workers and professional men—have found work. The remaining eighty per cent—farmers, unskilled laborers, the aged and the sick—are still in camps, reduced to the apathy, bitterness and resentment produced by refugee camp life everywhere. Living on the dole, kept officially segregated from the local population, most of the refugees have had scant opportunity for work or study (though there has been encouraging growth of community development and vocational training programs in Gaza), and little hope for the future. With their grievances and their swelling numbers, the refugees have been a standing invitation to manipulation by demagogues. They are a volatile, highly inflammable population in a region where the fires are banked but still smoking.

Inevitably, the life of Arabs in Israel is strongly colored by the presence of refugees across the frontier. The Arab states continue to press for the return of all refugees to Israel, but have consistently refused to end their war against her. Israel has repeatedly offered to negotiate all differences with the neighboring Arab governments still at war with her, but refuses to consider the refugee problem separately and apart from a general settlement. And there the matter has rested, with the United Nations spending twenty million dollars a year on an international force to maintain the uneasy truce, and the United States, Britain and Canada paying ninety per cent of the support of the refugees in the camps.

Of the Arabs who remain in Israel, nearly two-thirds live in villages. There are a hundred and three villages, many of them far beyond the roads, perched on the rocky hillsides—clusters of simple, single-story stone or adobe houses, whitewashed or sometimes painted a light blue to ward off evil. From the walls just below the flat roofs, the end of an occasional stout pole projects, as in the American Southwest. The villages are apt to be dirty and rich in flies, but the slender minaret and shallow dome of even the shabbiest village mosque has a classical Moslem simplicity in attractive contrast to the ugly concrete cubes that pass for architecture in much of Tel Aviv.

An Arab village

Street scene in Arab market in Nazareth

The narrow, roughly cobbled Arab village streets with their open drains are picturesque, but there is nothing charming in an infant mortality rate higher than necessary, or in tuberculosis, or in fewer and poorer schools than one would like. Only now are decent roads being built into many of the villages in the hills in place of tracks for the overburdened little donkeys. Electricity and some telephones, extended public health services, medical care and a growing number of schools are coming to the villages. Vital statistics are encouraging when

53

contrasted with those of other countries in the Middle East; but all is not rosy, and there is still a fair way to go.

Most Arab villages are near the country's frontiers, either in Galilee to the north where the only two Arab towns in the country, Shfar'am and Nazareth, are found or toward the eastern border or the coastal plain that forms the narrow waist of the country. Twenty-five thousand of the nomadic Arabs called Bedouins live in the desert to the south of Beersheba, where a splendid camel market serves them every Monday and Thursday morning. The rest of Israel's Arabs live in towns and cities where the population is mixed but predominantly Jewish: Jerusalem, Ramla, Lydda, Haifa, Acre, and Tel Aviv's sister

The Monday and Thursday morning Beersheba camel market

town of Jaffa. About half the Arabs are dependent on agriculture and fishing, and the other half earn a living as miners and craftsmen, in industry, commerce and service trades, with a number employed in the lower levels of the civil service.

The nation's Proclamation of Independence declares:

> The State of Israel . . . will maintain complete equality of social and political rights for all its citizens, without distinction of creed, race or sex. It will guarantee freedom of religion and conscience, of language, education and culture. It will safeguard the Holy Places of all religions . . .

In the first dozen years of independence, infant mortality among Arabs in Israel dropped from sixty-seven to forty-three per thousand (in Egypt next door, the United Nations reports it as over two hundred per thousand). Eighty per cent of the Israeli Arab children of school age now go to school—still not enough, but nearly twice as many as before independence. More and more Arab girls go to school, and Arab women vote, a thing unheard of in almost all the rest of the Middle East. Altogether, over ninety per cent of the Arab electorate has voted, and the last national legislature, the Knesset, elected three Arab Christians, three Moslems and one Druze.

The amount of Arab farmland now irrigated has increased fifteenfold since independence to seventy-five hundred acres, and eighty per cent of Arab farmers now own their own land. Their cattle have more than trebled. Arabs are members of Israel's highly developed labor unions, use their comprehensive medical services, and travel to Cyprus on inexpensive union tours. Both Arabic and English appear with Hebrew on Israel's postage stamps, coins, bank notes and street signs; Arabic, as well as Hebrew, is used in the Knesset; and as a language of instruction in Arab schools.

All this is fair treatment of a minority and heartening evi-

An Arab farmer plows his field

dence of the progress that minority is making. But there are still emotional and social barriers facing the Israeli Arab. According to the first qualified Israeli Arab sociologist, Baheej Khleif, the critical question facing his people is whether they will become, and feel themselves, completely accepted as Israelis. While there is almost no unemployment among Arab university graduates, and while the Israeli government ministries do employ Arab officers, it is Baheej Khleif's contention that most of these remain in humble posts. There is admitted difficulty in persuading the Jewish public to accept Arab civil servants; there is often automatic, if understandable, suspicion that the Arab is anti-Jewish.

Among the nine thousand students at Hebrew University and at the Haifa Technion there are now about a hundred and thirty Arabs—too few, but twice the number five years ago.

56

Khleif studied at Hebrew University, then on a Ford Foundation grant at The Hague's Institute of Social Studies which specializes in currents of change in the new nations. In his late twenties, he is coordinator for Arab student affairs in the trade union organization Histadrut, which should be a good place to work for Jewish-Arab reconciliation.

Khleif emphasizes that material well-being, even the obvious improvement in the Arab standard of living since Israel's independence, is far less important to Arab students than their emotional and psychological problems. "They are a minority which had been a majority . . . and their awareness of this is the underlying factor in their problem of adjusting to their status in modern Israel."

Khleif looks forward to the day when trained Israeli Arabs will take their place beside their Jewish fellows in Israel's Afro-Asian aid programs—an idea which should cause a healthy stir when it can be put into practice. Khleif has now twice represented his country at international conferences, identifying himself simply as an "Israeli Arab." When other Arab delegates urged him to call himself a "Palestinian Arab" instead, he says he told them to "stop burying their heads in the sand, and recognize the fact that the modern Middle East includes two hundred and thirty thousand Arabs who are citizens of Israel."

Now, the Israeli Arabs are isolated from the mainstream of Arab culture. The non-Arab but Moslem states of Turkey and Iran are friendly enough, as is the island republic of Cyprus which has a large Turkish Moslem population. Still, the majority of the forty million neighbors and members of the Arab League remain at war with Israel, and the others join in the general boycott and denunciation. Requests by Israel that her Moslem citizens be permitted to make the pilgrimage to Mecca and Medina have been refused by Saudi Arabia and

Jordan, through which the pilgrims would have to pass. An Arab in Israel who has made his peace with his government and is trying to live as a decent, law-abiding citizen is in danger of being branded traitor by his fellows across the frontier.

If the neighboring Arab states can bring themselves to recognize the existence of the State of Israel, and refrain from trying to strike at it through its Arab citizens, that would do a lot to ease the dilemma of Israeli Arabs, and help the effort being made by their government to make them a part of the nation.

The future of the Arabs and the other minorities who live in Israel is inextricably bound up with that of the Jewish majority. That future depends in great part on a general accord in the Middle East; in the resettlement of the Arab refugees who fled Palestine; in the acceptance of Israel as a nation state, with freedom for all citizens there to live and prosper. Then one could hope that, with the reclaiming of the desert, with better health and more education for her minorities and a continuing and important role for them in the government, Israel could become an example for a better way of life throughout the Middle East.

Harvesting wheat in the Negev

Chapter 4

THE LAND

The cheerful maps and guides which Israel prints for visitors, and the long black hired cars which carry them around bear the government tourist insignia: two stylized antique figures in robes, sandals and beards walking single file and carrying between them on their shoulders a pole from which hangs a bunch of grapes nearly as big as they are. These are the scouts whom Moses sent to "spy out the land of Canaan." After forty days they returned, bearing figs and pomegranates and grapes, saying, "We came unto the land whither thou sent us, and surely it floweth with milk and honey."

59

They were right. The Negev, now desert, was then flourishing. But over the last thousand years and more, the elaborate irrigation system of the ancient Idumeans and Nabateans fell into ruin, the pastures and the fields that once bore crops returned to waste and scrub. It has been hard work to make any of the land fertile again.

Now, after the struggles of the pioneer agricultural societies and the intensive efforts to redeem the Negev since Independence, the land begins to bloom again. Enough has been done to make green those parts which were little but rock and barren soil. One of the most exciting things in Israel is the prospect of seeing what will happen to the rest of the country over the next few years. Where Biblical Israel was usually bounded by the settlements of Dan in the north and Beersheba in the south, Beersheba with its modern buildings sprouting on the edge of the desert is now the capital of the Negev, and the gateway to the south. The half of Israel that lies below Beersheba stretches all the way down to King Solomon's copper mines at Timna and his port on the Red Sea nearby at Eilat. Former Prime Minister David Ben-Gurion has predicted a population of two million for the Negev, and it is just possible that, in this land of the impossible, the future will bear him out.

Sde Boker, the kibbutz of which Ben-Gurion is a member, sits on a windswept, yellowish-grey tableland not far from the high bluffs that rim the Dead Sea. Here, in what seems a sterile, lonely part of the world, fifty men and women—most of them young and most of whom could settle into a more comfortable life in the city any time they wanted to pack and move—have built their community houses and raised sheep and cattle, corn, tomatoes, watermelons, peaches, olives, grapes, figs, pomegranates. The frame houses and the grounds around them—not the fields—have the raw, half-finished look characteristic of much of Israel. A number of settlers were stationed nearby

The northern hills of Galilee

while doing their military service, and decided they would like to try to settle there. It is still enough of a wild frontier so that about a year ago a boy and a girl returning after dark from an excursion were waylaid and murdered by Bedouins for the few valuables they possessed. And it is typical of the pioneering spirit of the land—half Biblical visionary and half intensely practical and simple—that David Ben-Gurion is a sometime sheep-shearer in this community.

As the kibbutzim grow and prosper, they hive off, and younger members go out to start kibbutzim of their own. Also, as they get older, the kibbutzim tend to become less purely agricultural settlements, and more and more involved in light manufacturing of products such as plywood—a trend to industrialization that is true of the country as a whole.

Most of the settlements are clustered in the narrow waist of the country, and in Galilee in the north, and few and far between in the long triangle of the Negev south of Beersheba. Israel's climate is equable and Mediterranean, but there are variations: a dry, subtropical coastal plain, but with enough rain during the winter; the cooler and drier foothills and low mountains of central Israel rising to Jerusalem; the Jordan Valley which has a mild winter and a hot, dry summer with nearly tropical vegetation where the river winds through the lowest valley in the world on its way to the Dead Sea; and the dry, hot, hot desert of the Negev. In most places, most of the time, the weather is gentle. For a few days in the spring and again in the fall the hot wind, called the sharaf in Hebrew and hamsin in Arabic, blows in from the southern Arabian desert, and it is the custom to talk of it as if it were a blast from the

Inferno. But anyone used to summer in the American Middle West, let alone the burning plains of India, will find it, at most, a minor inconvenience. The winters, while not very cold, may strike the American visitor as raw and uncomfortable because of the lack of central heating.

Geographically, the land is divided into four zones. First there is the coastal plain from the Egyptian-held Gaza strip through the Tel Aviv region to a point just north of Haifa, a gently winding coastline of beaches and bluffs without natural harbors until one reaches Haifa, with sand dunes and lagoons and pools and water birds, and a railway that follows the coast north through Haifa to the Lebanese border and south all the way to Cairo.

View of Haifa from Mt. Carmel

Jordan River

The coastal plain is semi-arid but fertile, cut into a neat patchwork of fields in which the spray of sprinklers catches the sun. It is not only a "land of wheat and barley and vines and fig trees and pomegranates, a land of olive oil and honey," but it is now also a land of barley, millet and corn, and a land of melons, tomatoes, dates, bananas, cherries, and Jaffa oranges. The oranges are exported to Europe, as far north as Iceland where every man, woman and child eats more than fifteen pounds of them a year. Fish farming is popular and Israel's ponds produce more carp each year than does any other nation.

From the snowy slopes of Mount Hermon, which rises 9,232 feet on the Syria-Lebanon border a few miles to the north of the frontier, a mountain spine runs through Israel to Mount Sinai at the tip of the Sinai Peninsula of Egypt, where Moses received the Ten Commandments. A modest two thousand feet above sea level on the average, the hills of Samaria, Galilee and Judea slope gently to the coastal plain, but on the east, dip sharply, gullied and eroded, into the Jordan Valley.

Water from the Jordan River and the Sea of Galilee in the north and from the Yarkon River near Tel Aviv is piped to the northern Negev to help restore the fertility of the desert. With the Islamic conquest of the seventh century and the neglect that followed, sand blew in from the shore, and gradually the land became semi-desert. But traces of the ancient installations remain—the Pools of Solomon near Bethlehem, King Hezekiah's underground conduit some five feet tall that brought water to the Old City of Jerusalem (now in Jordan), the aqueducts of the Romans—and some of the old cisterns and reservoirs have been restored and put to use again.

The Jordan River flows from a spring on Mount Hermon through the marshes of Lake Hula, still some two hundred and thirty feet above sea level, down through the hills of Israel to

Sea of Galilee

the Sea of Galilee, nearly seven hundred feet below sea level. The Sea of Galilee is a fresh water lake some thirteen miles long, roughly heart-shaped, and three to seven miles wide. Here, fishermen still cast their nets as they did at the time of Christ and his apostles. Restaurants at the water's edge offer St. Peter's fish—a very tasty one alleged to be that in which the miraculous shekel with which to pay taxes was found in the Bible story. Overlooking Galilee is the Mount of the Beatitudes, and on the northern shore at Capernaum are the ruins of a second-century synagogue on a site where Jesus is thought to have preached.

In one church by the lake is a handsome old mosaic of the Multiplication of the Loaves and the Fishes. The whole lake is alive with memories of the stories of the New Testament: the apparition of Christ walking on the waters, Jesus preaching to the multitude from the lake, the Miraculous Draught of Fishes.

The Bible tells of a sudden storm on the Sea of Galilee which alarmed the apostles. Sudden chill winds blowing down the mountainsides, the massing of snow clouds, and the whipping of the dark water into dangerous waves still catch the traveler unexpectedly. Then, almost without warning, it will be over and one may see the warm late afternoon light over the Transjordanian Plateau, rising abruptly two thousand feet a few miles to the east, and to the north, Mount Hermon in the distance, like the top of a giant melted ice cream cone.

The fauna and flora in the region around the lake are among the most varied in this surprisingly rich country. There are

Ruins of the synagogue at Capernaum

many water birds here, both indigenous and migrants on the great air lanes between Asia, Africa and Europe: flamingos, pelicans, Indian darters and great herons, cormorants, demoiselle cranes, Siberian ringed plovers, and at least three species of kingfisher. There are wild boar and lynx and tawny foxes, too, around the Sea of Galilee, and wolves, gazelles, otters and porcupines. And all this among the vegetation typical of Galilee —bulrushes in the shallows of the waters, and in the hills pomegranate and locust trees, rhododendron, mignonette, and a pink oleander that grows to be twelve feet tall.

From the southern end of the lake the River Jordan curves past the green and wooded banks and the steps where generations of pilgrims have come to be baptized. It flows through Israel into Jordan. Slower now in mid-course but still a stream in size (somehow, I had pictured it as wide and stately, like the Ohio or the Mississippi), it meanders across the frontier and in wide loops down through the hot, nearly tropical Jordan valley, until it flows into the Dead Sea, thirteen hundred feet below sea level. This depression is part of the African Rift, a long

Wadi Masri, a part of the Great African Rift near Eilat

Salt Rock, "Lot's Wife"

crack in the earth's crust between two geological faults which commences in Syria and continues through the Sea of Galilee, the Jordan Valley and the Dead Sea, keeps right on going under the Red Sea and ends in East Africa in the region of the great African lakes. A place called Badwater in Death Valley, California, at two hundred and eighty feet below sea level is the lowest in the Western Hemisphere, but nothing can match the Dead Sea.

The Dead Sea is another thirteen hundred feet deep in spots, has no outlets, and is about seven times as salty as the Atlantic. It is impossible for a person to sink in the Dead Sea, and tourists ostentatiously float about reading newspapers. Israel extracts potash, bromide, magnesium and common salt from the water at Sodom on the south shore, where the Biblical Sodom and Gomorrah and three other cities of exceptional wickedness were destroyed by fire from heaven. It was near Sodom that Lot's wife was turned to a pillar of salt. She yielded to temptation

69

while fleeing and turned back to look at the destruction, in spite of the warning not to do so. Predictably, visitors are now shown a pillar of salt. There is also a small mountain of solid salt, thought to be a part of the bed of another salt lake in the past.

Most of Israel's minerals, except for iron ore in Galilee, are found in the Negev, from Sodom south: phosphates, manganese, potash, bromine, copper, feldspar, glass sand, kaolin and other clays, bitumen, granite and gypsum, and a little oil— enough to supply a small percentage of the country's needs. There is also a field of natural gas.

"Negev" means "south land" or "dry land." It looks like a wasteland. As you fly south, the sand begins just south of Tel Aviv and continues all the way to Egypt. The sandy gray of the northern Negev is sculptured in waves, giving way to grotesquely eroded limestone mountains, cut by deep gullies

Negev rock formations

through which run the whitish, boulder-strewn beds of the
wadies, dry water courses which turn to torrents during the infrequent rains. Seen from the air, the desert and the barren
mountains seem to stretch to infinity. The occasional blackish
pinheads below are bushes which can survive with almost no
rain; at long intervals, a star-shaped pattern with long strag-
gling rays indicates a water hole. The infrequent trucks or
jeeps on the tracks below raise clouds of dust like tawny
smokescreens.

Yet this is the land in which eighty thousand Israelis have
come to live, most of them in the last few years. This is Israel's
future. In Beersheba, the Desert Research Institute is experi-
menting with solar energy, the use of brackish water and the
adaptation to the Negev of plants brought from arid regions of
India and South Africa. Towns are sprouting on this unlikely
frontier, and with them, factories and new industries, roads and
fields. Here are the new settlers, and the excitement that comes
with creating a town of ten thousand like Dimona where less
than ten years ago there was only desert. The country is in love,
collectively, with its pioneers, and along with popular songs
celebrating the defense forces ("Our heads will not bend") and
Biblical themes ("Land flowing with milk and honey") are
ballads like "Simona from Dimona." The song goes on at some
length about Sodom and graphite and salt and Lot, but keeps
returning to Simona's healthy tan.

Like much apparently sterile soil, the loess of the northern
Negev can be made fertile—with water. And the remains of
flourishing cities like Avdat, capital of the ancient Nabateans,
south of Dimona, and Sde Boker are proof of what can be done
with intelligent use of the scanty resources at hand. Even now,
the southern desert supports a surprising amount of animal life
adapted to the dry heat. At night, the desert comes alive with
animals hidden during the heat of the day: sand rats and ger-

bils, jerboas and other small, shy rodents from burrows in the dunes—these last are prodigious jumpers like their cousins, the kangaroo rats of the American Southwest; fireflies, fire beetles and grubs, leopard moths and hawk moths; jackals and hyenas; horseshoe bats, pipestral bats and Egyptian fruit bats, white owls and eagle owls.

The settlers who come to this wild, desolate south, who find the life in the cities confining and oppressive, have their own deep satisfactions. First, there is nothing in the desert—nothing at all. Then, there are the hastily built simple houses and the

The Rock of Massada, the site of King Herod's castle

watchtower, the tank trucks bringing precious water over the new road. Then, the new pipeline to bring water to the new groves and fields and pastures. In time, as the community grows and is joined by others in the region, no doubt the more individual souls will strike out for new territory, until in the end all the Negev is settled and there will be a certain loneliness and nostalgia for the days before there were many people. Now, these are the pioneers, and the country is empty and spectacular. At sunset the light is reflected in a million metallic flecks on the sides of the barren mountains.

Chapter 5

THE BEGINNING

The first people known to have lived in the land that became Israel were cave men, not unlike the hulking, beetle-browed Neanderthal man of Europe and relatively sophisticated in their use of stone tools.

Much later, about four thousand years before Christ, the first Semites from southern Arabia reached the land where they lived as cave-dwelling herders and farmers; and they continued there until well after the time of Christ. The neatly dug-out prehistoric city outside Beersheba, the cliffside caves where the Dead Sea Scrolls and other ancient Hebrew manuscripts were found, and the caves in Nazareth where Joseph and Mary and the early Christians lived, are all part of the contemporary scene in the Holy Land.

Sometime between 2000 B.C. and 1500 B.C., a second wave of Semitic nomads moved northward from Arabia, among them the ancestors of Israel. They were led by the patriarchs Abraham, Isaac and Jacob, who settled first in the Euphrates Valley and came into Israel from the north. The difference between their people, the Hebrews, and the other nomads was a profound one, for they brought with them a religion in which man worshiped but one God instead of a multitude of competitive and hostile regional and tribal deities. It was this concept of monotheism that was the Hebrews' great legacy to the world. With this belief in one God grew the belief, as Dr. James Parkes, a wise Anglican student of Jewish and Christian theology, has put it, in a "link between the ethical conduct of a community

Dead Sea Scrolls on exhibit at Hebrew University

and divine guidance and approval, which marks the religious development of Israel during all her subsequent history."

Abraham, according to some interpretations, was known as Ibhri, or Hebrew, meaning "one who is from across"—this being in turn a reference to his coming from the city of Haran or Ur of the Chaldees, on the other side of the Euphrates River, in what is now northern Syria. The Bible tells how God gave Abraham's grandson Jacob the name of Israel, and how the twelve sons of Jacob were the traditional ancestors of the Twelve Tribes of Israel.

This patriarchal and nomadic society flourished, but then, after some centuries, there came a terrible drought. Following common nomadic practice, the Hebrews asked permission to graze their flocks in northeastern Egypt, near Israel.

In Egypt, the Hebrews were reduced to a state of servitude, until led by Moses, who forged them into one people, one nation, they returned to Israel about 1350 B.C. Bondage in Egypt under the Pharaohs and the epic of their return through the wild gorges and the starkly rearing red granite mountains of the Sinai peninsula made an unforgettable impression on the Hebrews. Their story of God's gift to Moses of the Law, at the center of which is an ethical foundation for the monotheism

75

which came to be shared by a great part of mankind. The Ten Commandments are still the basis of an ordered communal life for Jews, Christians and Moslems.

Gradually, after conquest of the Canaanites, the Israelites settled in the Promised Land. For a time they were ruled by a series of "judges" who arose in times of trouble to rally their people against the incursions of other tribes, still nomadic, seeking to displace them. Meanwhile, the Philistines, who had been driven out of Greece and the Aegean Islands, had founded a series of city states in the south of Palestine. About 1000 B.C., in danger of being conquered by the increasingly powerful Philistines, the Hebrew tribes in the kingdoms of Israel and Judah were united for the first time under a king, Saul. Saul was killed in battle with the Philistines, but his successor, King David, consolidated the state. He extended its frontiers and took the old Canaanite city of Urushalim as his capital, Jerusalem, at the center of the two Hebrew kingdoms, bringing the northern and southern tribes closer together. Under David, the shepherd boy Little David who in the Biblical songs and stories played on his harp and with his slingshot slew the Philistine champion Goliath, the kingdom enjoyed a simple, centralized administration in place of the more primitive tribal rule. There were national taxes and a standing army. The country was strong, stable and prosperous. And there were two developments in literature of the greatest importance to the world of David and to all who were to come after him: history as we understand it, as a literal record relatively free of embroidery and improvement (as in the Biblical account of the revolt of Absalom); and religion as a deeply personal and individual experience, as recorded in the early Psalms.

David felt himself to be unworthy because he had "shed blood," but he asked his son Solomon to build a temple at Jerusalem for the Ark of the Covenant, the wooden box housing

Site of the Biblical Sodom

the two tablets inscribed with the Ten Commandments. Solomon, the legendary wisest of all men and the poet of the Song of Songs, built the great temple in Jerusalem. His caravans traveled the Silk Route through Central Asia to China, and his ships sailed to Africa and the Far East from his port near Eilat on the Red Sea. Nearby, he mined copper for exchange with gold from the Ophir of the Bible (nobody is sure now exactly where Ophir was). It was from Ethiopia that the Queen of Sheba came to visit Solomon, through Eilat. The Ethiopians believe that Sheba bore Solomon a child who became the ancestor of the rulers of Ethiopia, which explains the line of Hebrew across the arms of Ethiopia. As a revival of this

77

Ethiopian ship offloading at Eilat

ancient connection, in Eilat now one can see ships from the Eritrean coast of Ethiopia, their names in Amharic lettering on their sterns, loading cargo for the Israeli-Ethiopian trade.

On the death of Solomon, the nation was split in two, with ten tribes in the kingdom of Israel in the north, and the remaining two tribes in the kingdom of Judah, including the city of Jerusalem, to the south. But the independence of this small nation, even when united, depended in great part on the relative strength or weakness of the great empires who were her neighbors, Egypt to the south, Assyria to the northeast and Babylonia to the southeast. The kingdom of Israel was conquered in the middle of the eighth century B.C. by Sargon, King of Assyria,

78

and Judah was conquered in 586 B.C., Solomon's Temple destroyed, and its people carried off into captivity by Nebuchadnezzar, King of Babylonia.

Fifty years later, under the relatively benevolent rule of the Assyrian Empire by the Persian Cyrus, some of the grandchildren of the captive Judeans, or Jews, were permitted to return from exile, and at Jerusalem rebuilt their Temple. It was a time of great rejoicing, a time when a Hebrew way of life directly followed the Ten Commandments and the teachings of the Hebrew prophets. But in about two centuries, the country—always the crossroads between the continents, always the buffer state—was conquered by Alexander the Great, and there followed a period of Hellenizing influence, the building of Greek cities, the spread of the Greek language, and finally, the suppression of the Hebrew religion. Jewish observances were forbidden. The Temple at Jerusalem was desecrated with an altar to the Greek gods.

Led by the Maccabees, the Jews revolted in 168 B.C. (there is at West Point a bas-relief of their leader, Judah the Maccabee, a brilliant guerrilla warrior), and for nearly a century an independent state of Judea was ruled by Maccabean kings and princes. The Feast of Hannukah in the fall each year commemorates the restoration of the Temple: for eight days in each Jewish household one candle is lit until all are burning, and the public places throughout Israel are bright with light. It was during these years that the books which were to form the Old Testament were selected from the voluminous archives of Hebrew scriptures, most of which had been written much earlier.

In 63 B.C., Jerusalem was conquered by the Roman legions. But even with the loss of independence, there continued a school centered in Galilee which interpreted the laws of Moses and preached the coming of a Savior.

Within the lifetimes of the children and the grandchildren of the children who played in Judea at the time of the Roman conquest, there arose in Nazareth a teacher called Yeshu by the Jews and Jesus by the Greeks. His Sermon on the Mount and other teachings in Galilee were the beginnings of the new, reformed religion, Christianity. The Judeo-Christian faith and the later acceptance by Mohammed of this as a major source of his still newer religion of Islam were to make of this small part of the earth a land which could be called truly the Holy Land.

Ruins of stone columns at the Roman port of Caesarea

At first all went well under the Romans. Herod the Great was somewhat less illustrious than his title, and as kings in Judea, the Herods were completely subservient to their Roman masters. But they created the splendid port of Caesarea and built the Second Temple in Jerusalem with magnificent sanctuaries, courts and terraces. Meanwhile in the north there was unrest among the people of Galilee who expected a Messiah. A sharpening series of conflicts between the Roman colonial authorities and the recently independent Jews, erupted in

66 A.D. into full-scale warfare with Rome. In the turbulence, comparatively little attention was paid to the teaching and crucifixion of Jesus of Nazareth.

For three years the Jewish commonwealth managed to hold off the Romans. Then, in 70 A.D., under the Roman emperor Titus, Jerusalem was besieged, taken and sacked, and the Temple destroyed. Nothing was left except a short length of the foundation now known as the Wailing Wall. Hundreds of thousands of Jews perished in the defeat or were transported as slaves to other parts of the Roman Empire.

Sixty-two years later, the Jews rose once more in the last struggle of their times for a land of their own. They held Jerusalem again for three years, but finally, they were routed. Before the Romans took them, many committed suicide in caves in the cliffs beside the Dead Sea. As one flies over the salt sea now, one can see in the cliffs the entries to the caves where Bar Kochba, the Jewish leader, conducted his last, hopeless resistance and was finally overcome in 135 A.D.

There followed the long saga of the Diaspora when the Jews were scattered across the world. The deportations carried them to Mesopotamia and Rome and Egypt, Kurdistan and the Caucasus. Through the centuries they became wanderers over the world. There was now no Jewish political center, no religious hierarchy, for every community was autonomous. The extraordinary thing is that they did not disappear as a people, were not absorbed by the many countries in which they lived, but managed somehow to retain their identity—it seems above all because of their refusal to abandon their religion. Yet because the Jews, as aliens, survived on sufferance with few of the rights of others, and because they themselves remained apart, clinging to their own ways, their own standards, they were regarded with suspicion. They were convenient scapegoats in times of trouble, tempting prey to autocrats and governments who needed to raise money in a hurry. During the Middle Ages and after, Jews were confined to ghettoes in the great cities where they were restricted to a few occupations. They earned the reputation of being unwilling to work with their hands on the land. They worked harder than most people, and this did not make them popular. In the darkest days, god-fearing folk were warned against them as monsters who killed Christian babies to use their blood in unholy rituals. The religious passions which were inflamed (still smoldering in some parts of the world) ended in the tortures of the Inquisition.

The Jews in exile were driven from Spain in 1492, and from Portugal in 1496. They were long forbidden to settle in many European countries, including England, and I remember my insular astonishment at hearing my Shakespearean professor at Princeton suggest that this was a major reason for the portrait of Shylock in *The Merchant of Venice*.

The Jews who have come to modern Israel were born in a hundred countries and more. Earlier, they had lived in the Republic of Venice and the Transvaal Republic, the Republic of Texas, Montenegro, Serbia and a hundred nations which no longer exist. But, by some miracle, the Jewish nation does. Today about a sixth of all the Jews in the world live in Israel. A slightly larger number lives in New York City, and about half of all the Jews in the world live in the United States and Canada.

Roman theater in Caesarea

Chapter 6

THE CONQUERORS

For two thousand years there was nowhere an independent Jewish government. In the thirteen centuries after its defeat, the land was invaded, pillaged, colonized and reconquered fourteen times. For the five hundred years between the death of Bar Kochba, 135 A.D., and the time of the Moslem conquest, 636 A.D., the land of Palestine, as the country was now called, was ruled as a Roman colony. Under tolerant rulers like Septimus Severus and Alexander Severus, the Jews and Christians of Palestine were treated with respect; Alex-

84

ander was said to have put statues of both Christ and Moses in his own chapel. In the Jewish communities which survived in the Holy Land, especially in Galilee, the Hebrew sacred texts of the Mishnah (Instruction) and most of the Jerusalem Talmud (Research) were completed by 400 A.D. During the following two hundred years, the Eastern Christian churches flourished, and Palestine became the goal of many thousands of European Christian pilgrims. As a part of the Eastern Roman Empire with its center at Byzantium, later called Constantinople and then Istanbul, Palestine probably supported a larger population than it has at any time until very recent years. Jerusalem was one of the richest cities of the East.

Yet for most of the people who lived in Palestine, the burden of provincial taxation was crushing, and imperial rule cruel and capricious. Government was largely incompetent. Trade declined. There was savage persecution, now of Christians, now of Jews and the allied Samaritans. Finally, when a heretic-hunting version of Christianity was accepted as the state religion, the Jews were reduced to a miserable second-class citizenship, barred from the professions and public office, forbidden to build synagogues, and left to the mercy of mob violence. It is not surprising that several thousand Jews willingly joined the Persians in their invasion of the eastern provinces in 614 A.D.

The Persian occupation of Palestine lasted until 628 A.D. when the territory was reconquered by the Byzantines. By 636 A.D., only four years after the death of the Prophet Mohammed, the Arabs defeated the Byzantines and took Palestine. All along the frontiers of the Mediterranean world barbarian and nomadic tribes were pressing inward from the inhospitable deserts of the south and the mountains of the north to the fertile, cultivated lands. The Byzantine and Persian empires were exhausted, and the vineyards and the fields of grain, the flocks and herds of Palestine were tempting. The

Byzantine mosaic showing cross with fish and pomegrana

population—mostly Christians and Jews in Palestine—were disaffected after centuries of misrule and offered little resistance.

The Arab conquerors, like the Romans, were relatively humane at first. The tribute they levied was no more than the old imperial tax. They were uninterested in their subjects' religion or how they ordered their own affairs. It is reported that the first Arab Caliph, Abu-Bakr, ordered his army: "Be just, for the unjust never prosper. Be valiant: die rather than retreat. Keep your word, even to your enemies. Be merciful: slay neither the old, nor the young, nor the women. Destroy no fruit trees, no crops, no beasts. Kill neither sheep, nor oxen nor camels, except it be for food." His successor, the Caliph Omar, who conquered Persia and Byzantium, including Palestine, is remembered for his simplicity and generosity. Islam called on Moslems to protect both Jews and Christians as "people of the Book." For the first hundred years, the Arab governing minority was forbidden to own land. And the land was farmed by the same peasants as before, for the nomadic Arab looked down on farmers and farming.

In the Arab world at the time, Moslems paid only a tax to help the poor; the great revenues needed to maintain the government were paid by non-Moslems. Later, when a fair proportion of the population had embraced Islam, as it had earlier been converted to Judaism and Christianity, there were far fewer to pay. Arabs were now permitted to own land, and inevitably a great deal of it passed into the hands of landowners, leaving the peasant farmer even poorer than before. Standards of agriculture continued to decline; conservation of water and the extensive irrigation which had given the land its fertility was neglected and then abandoned. Dr. Parkes comments: "The busy cities, the caravans of merchants, the thriving forests, the prosperous estates, and the rural industries with which Jesus or the apostles would have been familiar, have perished beneath the combined assaults of the Bedouin, the goat and the tax collector."

In the tenth century, control of Palestine passed to Egyptian rulers who claimed descent from Mohammed's daughter Fatima. In 1009, the Caliph al-Hakim ordered churches and synagogues in Palestine destroyed, and forbade Christian and Jewish pilgrimages. He spared the Church of the Nativity at Bethlehem, but destroyed the Church of the Holy Sepulchre built over Christ's supposed burial place in Jerusalem, and this produced violent reactions in Europe that ended in the Crusades to regain Christian access to the Holy Land. It also led to the spread of the tale and wide belief in Europe that it was the Jews who had somehow incited the Moslems to destroy this

The Crusaders' Wall at Acre

holy place, and there was a wave of massacres and of forced baptisms of Jews.

The call of Pope Urban II in 1095 to reopen the way to Jerusalem was the signal of the first of four Crusades. For over two centuries the monarchs, nobles and knights of much of Europe engaged in a series of wars against the Moslem rulers of the Holy Land, and often between themselves, allied with one or another of their supposed enemies. Jerusalem was captured on the fifteenth of July in 1099. All Jews and Moslems found within the city were killed.

The knights came from Sicily, from Provence, Lorraine and Normandy, from the Italian city states of Venice, Genoa and Pisa, from England, Germany, Hungary, Austria and Norway. Two kings of England, Richard I and Edward I, and Philip Augustus, King of France, took part in the Crusades. Frederick Barbarossa, Emperor of the Holy Roman Empire, died leading a Crusade. But what began with high courage and religious exaltation quickly lapsed into a petty struggle for place and profit among the leaders of the crusading armies. The inhabitants of Palestine lived through yet another period of weak, divided government and misrule.

The Kingdom of Jerusalem ruled an area that included what is now Lebanon in the north and stretched down to the Gulf of Aqaba. It was to survive for about a century, a feudal European kingdom on the western rim of Asia, and linger on in a ghostly way for a further century until the last Crusaders had been driven back to Europe.

The King of Jerusalem was responsible for the safety of all the kingdom, but Crusaders' baronies within it, the Church's military orders and other establishments, and colonies of Italian traders could act independently of his authority, with their own courts, free from tolls, making war or peace with the common enemy as it suited them. Groups of Crusaders were betrayed by other groups. The Orders of the Knights Templars and Knights Hospitallers were founded to care for pilgrims who were sick and to defend them on the road to Jerusalem. These two Orders appealed to the imagination of Europe, and they became vastly rich. In the end, they also became arrogant and little interested in the poor of the Kingdom of Jerusalem. When, in 1187, the Kingdom was conquered and its knights all but annihilated by the Kurdish general Saladin in Galilee at the Horns of Hittin, the Orders refused to give up a part of their treasure to pay a moderate ransom demanded for the poorer European Christians of the territory.

In the Christian world, the final division had already come between the Pope and the Patriarch, between Rome and Constantinople, between the Western and Eastern churches. They seemed as often enemies as allies. The Crusades, which had begun with an ugly sideshow in which one Peter the Hermit led a mob through Europe pillaging and massacring the Jews in its path, were increasingly debased. The word "crusade" was used to describe suppression of public protest, to attack rival Christian sects, to raise money for the religious authorities. The movement reached some sort of climax in 1212, the year of the two Children's Crusades, one of which reached Paris, and one the Italian ports before the survivors were released from their vows, and straggled home—not sold as slaves in Alexandria, as legend has it, but robbed and sometimes murdered, falling ill and dying by the wayside—a terrible and pathetic story.

The last of the Crusaders was driven from the Holy Land in 1303, ending two centuries of unhappy struggle. What was left in the end was the magnificent series of castles that still guard the heights throughout Israel, Jordan, Lebanon and Syria; and that relic of Crusaders' adopted Eastern dress, the neck flap hanging from the back of a knight's helmet to prevent his being seared by the sun striking his chain mail.

View of Kibbutz Yehi-Am from Crusader Castle

Always, there was a remnant of the Jewish nation in the land which was to become Israel, but most of Jewry was now scattered from Ethiopia to China and beyond. Each year on Yom Kippur, the Day of Atonement, they prayed, "Next year in Jerusalem!"

Meanwhile, the Promised Land of the Hebrews knew successive conquerors. After the Egyptians, the Phoenicians, the

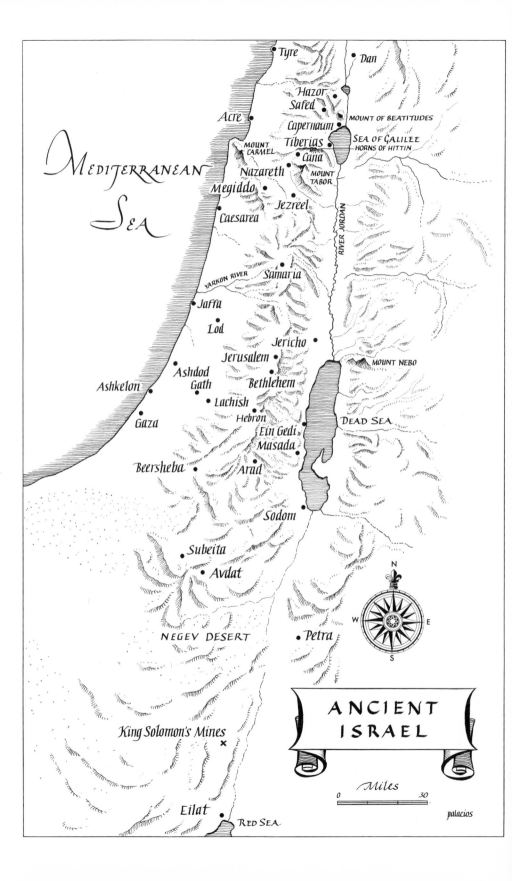

Romans, the Byzantine Christians, there was worse to come. For forty years ending in 1247, Turkish Tartars ravaged the country, sacking Jerusalem and massacring, in their turn, all the Christians who were found there. Then came the Mamluks, an extraordinary line of forty-seven Turkish and Circassian slaves who held the throne of Egypt for 267 years ending in 1517, by which time, it is estimated, they had reduced the population of Egypt, Syria and Palestine by two-thirds.

The Mongols under Hulagu Khan, a grandson of Genghis Khan, invaded the country in 1260. Then in 1400 came Tamerlane, another descendant of Genghis Khan, whose horsemen like those of his ancestor, pillaged from China through India and Arabia as far as Eastern Europe.

In 1517 came the Osmanli Turks whose rule of Palestine was to last almost uninterruptedly for four hundred years. What had once been an obscure province of Rome was now an obscure province of the Turks' Ottoman Empire, in its latter years perhaps one of the sorriest examples of misrule and inefficiency in all the long and melancholy history of imperialism. It ended in 1917 when the Turks who had joined the Germans were defeated in Palestine by the British under General Allenby. Numbers of Jews who had fled Palestine to avoid Turkish military service joined the Allied armies, among them a future Prime Minister, David Ben-Gurion, and a future President, Yitzchak Ben-Zvi, who in the United States volunteered for service with the five thousand Americans and Canadians, Argentinians and others with the Jewish Legion, sailing to fight under Allenby and their own Jewish commanders. Their insignia was the Star of David, and the ancient Hebrew pledge, "If I forget thee, O Jerusalem." It was the first time since the defeat of Bar Kochba by the Romans in 135 A.D. that the Jews had been able to fight under their own colors for their own homeland.

Chapter 7

RETURN TO ZION

Before the First World War was over, the British government, considering a number of different arguments in favor of the Zionist proposals, and anxious to show its gratitude to Chaim Weizmann for his brilliant work in synthesizing acetone for the Admiralty, sent, at Weizmann's suggestion, to Lord Rothschild, leader of the British Jewish community, the celebrated Balfour Declaration. This simple "declaration of sympathy with Jewish Zionist aspirations" by the Secretary of State Arthur James Balfour, not much over a hundred words long, brought jubilation to the Jewish world. It stated:

> His Majesty's Government view with favour the establishment in Palestine of a national home for the Jewish people, and will use their best endeavours to facilitate the achievement of this object, it being clearly understood that nothing shall be done which may prejudice the civil and religious rights of existing non-Jewish communities in Palestine, or the rights and political status enjoyed by Jews in any other country.

The Balfour Declaration was formally approved by France, Italy and the United States. Like many other carefully worded statements, it was still possible to misunderstand, and in 1922, Winston Churchill, then Colonial Secretary, felt obliged to

94

spell out the British position. In the "Churchill White Paper" he wrote:

> Unauthorised statements have been made to the effect that the purpose in view is to create a wholly Jewish Palestine. Phrases have been used such as that Palestine is to become "as Jewish as England is English." His Majesty's Government view any such expectation as impracticable and have no such aim in view. Nor have they at any time contemplated, as appears to be feared by the Arab Delegation [to the Palestine Arab Congress] the disappearance or the subordination of the Arab population, language or culture in Palestine. They would draw attention to the fact that the terms of the Declaration referred to do not contemplate that Palestine as a whole should be converted into a Jewish National Home, but that such a home should be founded *in Palestine.*

In other words, the British did not propose second-class citizenship for the Arab population of Palestine; and implicitly, the rights of Arabs and other non-Jewish citizens were to be protected. But Britain still believed in the creation of a Jewish homeland in Palestine.

Chaim Weizmann

Immigrants from North Africa disembark at Haifa

As a result of the First World War, the old Turkish province of Palestine was given to Britain to administer under a League of Nations mandate. The mandate quoted the Balfour Declaration in full, and went on to recognize "the historical connection of the Jewish people with Palestine and the grounds for reconstituting their national home in that country." It made Britain "responsible for placing the country under such political, administrative and economic conditions as will secure the establishment of the Jewish national home." It asked the mandatory power to "facilitate Jewish immigration" and to encourage "close settlement on the land."

Unfortunately, the mandate was far less clear about the position of Palestine's Arab majority. Under the British, the Jewish Agency, a social service organization, creating for the Jewish community, everything from better schools to help with immigration, was accepted by the mandatory government as liaison with that community, and made responsible for much administration. Proposals for an Arab agency or a council on which Arab leaders would sit came too late, and Arab leaders in Palestine were left with no executive responsibility for their own people at the same time that fellow Arabs had achieved independence or internal self-government in 1,200,000 square miles neighboring on Palestine. Palestine covered 10,000 square miles.

At first things seemed to go well. The Arabs had no objection to Jewish immigration, and the Arab leader Emir Feisal of Arabia wrote after the Balfour Declaration: "We feel that the Arabs and the Jews are cousins in race, having suffered similar oppressions at the hands of powers stronger than themselves . . . We Arabs, especially the educated among us, look with the deepest sympathy on the Zionist movement . . . We wish the Jews a most hearty welcome home." The Jewish leaders at the 1921 Zionist Congress spoke of "the determination of the Jewish people to live with the Arab people on terms of concord and mutual respect, and together with them to make the common home into a flourishing community." During the first years of the mandate, encouraging progress was made in common ventures with the Arabs, particularly in agriculture and organized labor (David Ben-Gurion was then a labor organizer).

The British government believed that it could keep its promises to both Jews and Arabs, reconcile the legitimate aspirations of both, and that during the temporary mandate, it could create a harmonious state in which both could live. But the British underestimated, as had the League of Nations, the depth of Arab opposition beneath the surface. It was felt—or at least the mandatory government acted as though it felt—that there was all the time in the world to bring the Arab society out of the feudal stagnation of four centuries of Turkish rule. The

British were content to await a naturally evolving partnership
between the Arabs and the European Jews who were planning
a cooperative society, emphasizing education, medicine and
public health, enthusiastically going back to the land, and
storming their problems as though they were an enemy
position.

Matters were complicated by some of the men sent out by
the British Colonial Office who found it easier dealing with the
Palestinian Arabs under a system of direct rule in the familiar
paternal colonial pattern, than with the European Jewish
society which in many ways was embarrassingly advanced, and
whose members often were as well or better educated than they
themselves. Some of the officers made no secret of their sympathy with the Arab majority. Then the administrative ma-
chinery itself was infernally complicated. There were religious
courts with wide powers, independent of the administration.
And the administration was not a government, but answered
to London which answered to the League of Nations at Geneva.
It was the administration's duty to serve and to govern two conflicting communities, with insufficient authority, and probably
without the necessary insight and imagination.

Increasingly, as the years of the mandate wore on, the British
government supported the Arabs. Sir Herbert Samuel, first
British High Commissioner in Palestine and himself a Jew, had
appointed Haj Amin al-Husseini as Mufti of Jerusalem and
President of the Supreme Moslem Council.

It was a disastrous choice. The Moslems remained suspicious
of Sir Herbert's and the British government's impartiality, and
the Mufti went on to fan the flames of religious fanaticism to
his personal political ends. He raised the cry that the Jews had
designs on the mosques of Jerusalem; in the thirties he used
both blackmail and assassination to silence Arab moderates
and drive the Arab side to increasingly violent agitation against
the Jews in Palestine. With a guerrilla army of five thousand

operating out of the hills of Galilee, the Mufti attacked Jewish settlements and terrorized the countryside. It seems incredible that in a country as small as Palestine a resolute government could not have run the Mufti's men to earth. But guerrillas are elusive and the government's inadequately armed forces were barely sufficient to protect the main roads, let alone the isolated Jewish settlements. In 1936, the Mufti launched a general strike of Arab workers, a campaign of civil disobedience and non-payment of taxes, and a boycott of the Jews. His saboteurs did a careful, professional job of blowing up most of Jaffa's old town. The Mufti had to flee Palestine. He continued his career in Hitler's headquarters, raising battalions for the Nazis.

In the years just before the Second World War the British found themselves in a dilemma. Intimidated to a degree by the rising Arab threats against the Jews, they were acutely aware of Palestine's growing strategic importance in the great struggle which was to come. Palestine covered vital supply lines between Asia and Britain and America, and it lay conveniently close to the sources of Russian oil in the Caucasus. Possession of Palestine helped block Germany from linking up with her partner Japan. Palestine became a stop on the air route to India.

All this helps to explain, if not justify, how Britain came to make the decision she then made. In May of 1939, on the eve of the war in which she was to fight for her own survival, Britain published a White Paper in which Jewish immigration into Palestine was to be strictly limited to ten thousand persons a year for five years, with an additional twenty-five thousand Jewish refugees to be admitted if it seemed necessary, but with no more Jewish immigration beyond this unless the Arabs, most improbably, should agree to it. There were also severe restrictions on purchase of land by Jews in Palestine.

The White Paper stunned the Jewish communities of the world. It is true that, in the hope and idealism of the days following the First World War, Britain had accepted the mandate for Palestine without being able to foresee the sudden desperate need for Jewish immigration when Hitler came to power in Germany fifteen years later. After the First World War, the Jews in Europe were thought to be protected by reliable minority treaties.

When the news first came of the Nazi plan for systematic destruction of the Jews of Europe, it was treated by the British Foreign Office as most unlikely. If this now seems tragically blind to what was happening in the world, it is fair to remember the incredulousness with which many in the United States received stories of what the Nazis planned to do to those Jews within their reach—stories of what they were already doing. Even some twenty years later, during the trial in Israel of Adolph Eichmann for crimes against the Jewish people and humanity, the picture that emerged of a powerful modern state engaged in the relentless pursuit and extermination of an entire people seemed hardly credible, though documented beyond any doubt. It seemed fantastic that any group of human beings could bring themselves to act in a way so inhuman. Yet the record was clear. And Hitler had told the world unmistakably what he intended to do.

If few others in 1939 could believe what was to come, the plan was clear to the Jews in the threatened European countries, to many of their relatives and friends overseas, and to the Zionists trying to bring their fellows to a refuge in Palestine. By this time more than a million Jews in Germany, Austria and Czechoslovakia were caught by the Nazi machine. Before the outbreak of war, Britain accepted nearly one hundred thousand refugees from Europe, most of them Jewish, but there was not much hope that England, the United States and other countries would permit further substantial immigration. The White Paper which closed the door in Palestine meant that for most Eastern European Jews escape was blocked.

Publication of the White Paper produced strong reaction.

The Mandates Commission of the League of Nations ruled that it did not carry out the terms of the mandate. A Zionist Congress repudiated it, and announced that the Jewish Agency would not cooperate in its enforcement. An Anglo-American Committee in 1946 produced a report which supported the admission by Palestine of a hundred thousand refugees, a plan U. S. President Harry S. Truman had called for several times. Jewish leaders were now grimly determined, one way or another, legally or illegally, to save as many people from Hitler as possible, and somehow get them to Palestine.

While the Jews totally rejected the British White Paper, at the same time they clearly recognized that Britain was the leader of the democracies in the war against the totalitarian states. Their leaders declared, "We shall fight the war as if there were no White Paper. But we shall fight the White Paper as if there were no war." Nearly thirty thousand Jews from Palestine volunteered for service with the British Army, even though little news of the Jewish forces was printed in the Palestine press, and troops returning home were obliged to remove the Star of David insignia from their uniforms and vehicles lest these offend the sensibilities of the Arabs. About twelve thousand Arabs enlisted, including many who came from outside Palestine. Of the Jewish volunteers, many were trained for special service in wholly Jewish units, serving as commandos in Syria and Iraq and Ethiopia, and parachuted behind the lines in Europe. More than half of these commando groups gave their lives.

The Nazi invasion of Poland which led to a declaration of war by Britain and France meant that another three million Jews had fallen into the hands of Hitler or were refugees in Russian-held territory. Desperate efforts were made to get survivors to Palestine. The British enforced the White Paper as though it were the mandate, turning back shiploads of refugees to quarantine on the island of Cyprus, near Palestine,

A cargo ship arrives in Israel with immigrants

or Mauritius, in the Indian Ocean off East Africa. Men barely out of their teens ran the blockade in old cargo ships, anything that would float, in an effort to bring a few thousand more concentration camp inmates to refuge.

More than a year after the war was over, a quarter of a million Jews were still held in German and Austrian camps. Then a ship carrying a large number of refugees from the camps was intercepted, and the unhappy people were returned to the camp life in Germany they had been trying to escape. Feeling ran high. It should be remembered here, that at this time, under mandatory law, possession of even small weapons for self-defense, by Jews or anyone else, was punishable by death. In Palestine, the White Paper and the mandate administration was fought not only by the Haganah, the Jewish Defense Force organized to protect settlements from raids by the Mufti's marauders, but also by groups of terrorists like the Irgun and Stern gangs who used assassination, bombing, hanging and booby-trapping as their weapons. Terrorism brought repressive countermeasures by the Palestine government, which led to even more violent acts of terrorism, and ever harsher countermeasures by the authorities. The moderates among the Arabs (it seems hard to remember now, but there had been a number of them, and some of them in positions of authority) had been effectively overridden by the Mufti, and now the Jewish Agency was no longer able to restrain the Jewish extremists. In the early summer of 1946, all of the leading Agency officers and two thousand other Jews were arrested and interned. Once the leaders, with the moderates among them, had been removed, Jewish terrorists blew up a wing of the King David Hotel in Jerusalem, killing a hundred persons including almost half of the British senior staff. The Zionist cause, already injured by the increasing violence and terrorism of its extremist supporters, was badly hurt by this outrage.

By 1947, the mandate government in Jerusalem was living behind barbed wire; administration had all but broken down. New agricultural settlements, new industries for the immigrants were still being created by the Jewish Agency, but against the greatest odds. The British government, which as early as 1937 had publicly come to the conclusion that the mandate was unworkable, again reached the same conclusion, and proposed turning the whole matter over to the United Nations.

It was the unanimous recommendation of the United Nations fact-finding committee that the mandate be terminated and Palestine made independent. Most of the committee favored economic union but political partition into separate Arab and Jewish states. On the initiative of the United States and with the agreement of the Soviet Union, the General Assembly approved this recommendation. Britain announced she would give up her responsibility for the mandate at midnight on May 14, 1948, but since she had not the agreement of both the Jews and the Arabs, refused assistance to the United Nations in making arrangements for partition and an orderly

David Ben-Gurion

transfer of power. The Arabs refused to have anything to do with the plan, refusing to accept only a part of Palestine.

At four o'clock in the afternoon of May 14, 1948, at the Tel Aviv Museum of Art, a few hours before the British mandate was to end at midnight, David Ben-Gurion wearing an unaccustomed dark suit and tie, proclaimed the State of Israel. Eleven minutes after the mandate ended, Israel was recognized by the United States, by Guatemala the next day, and shortly after, by the Soviet Union. Thus, fifty years after Theodor Herzl at the Zionist Congress at Basel in Switzerland had dreamed of the re-creation of a Jewish state in the ancient homeland, Israel was reborn. It was nearly nineteen hundred years since the Roman destruction of Jerusalem; nearly twenty-five hundred years since the destruction of the First Temple and the exile in Babylon; perhaps four thousand years since the Hebrew tribes had first reached the Promised Land. The proclamation of independence was accompanied by the simultaneous invasion of forces from five neighboring countries sworn to destroy the new state. But at last it existed, a homeland and a refuge from persecution for Jews from anywhere in the world. It existed and could be defended.

Raising the Israeli flag on the shores of the Gulf of Aqaba

Chapter 8

INDEPENDENCE

Three times during the night of May 14, the first night of the State of Israel's independence, Tel Aviv was bombed by the Egyptian Air Force. The bombers came back four times in the next two days. The day after the mandate ended, the Arab League's Secretary-General, Abdur-Raham Assam Pasha, told a press conference in Cairo: "This will be a war of extermination and a momentous massacre which will be spoken of like the Mongolian massacres and the Crusades."

Looking back, it seems miraculous that Israel survived. The five invading Arab armies were trained and well-equipped.

Against their thirty thousand men was the Haganah, a partially-trained Israeli defense force of about twenty thousand men and women who had drilled secretly at night before the end of the mandate. Only some sixty per cent of the Haganah forces were armed. Three thousand—a third of them girls—formed the Palmach, tough, trained commandos known as "Samson's Foxes." Many of them had served with the British. There were a few artillery pieces (one for the defense of Jerusalem), some ammunition, a good part of which the Israelis had made themselves, a few machine guns and homemade armored trucks, some grenades and Molotov cocktails. There were no heavy machine guns, and neither anti-tank nor anti-aircraft guns. The Israeli Air Force was mainly Piper Cubs.

Britain maintained until the very end the blockade against further Jewish immigration. The United States declared an embargo against the sale of arms to the new state. Military analysts, governments and friends of Israel, including many of the Zionist leaders in other countries, were pessimistic over the new state's chances of survival. It is doubtful if they or most of the Israelis caught up in the job of defending their country were aware in those first few days and weeks of just how close the Jewish people in Israel were to annihilation. Ben-Gurion and a few of the Israeli leaders knew.

The people of Israel—whether they came from those pioneering families fired with the idealism which had carried them through four and more generations of hard work in their efforts to re-create the Promised Land, or from the bedeviled refugees who found themselves in Israel because they had no place else to go—shared a desperate courage compounded of long years of abiding faith in the face of persecution, and of the knowledge that all of them, the whole nation, were literally fighting for their lives. Israel was a few miles wide, and its enemies had promised to push the Israelis into the sea. There was no reason to doubt they meant it.

Gertrude Samuels of *The New York Times,* a biographer of Ben-Gurion, has justly compared the courage of the Israelis under attack to that of the Londoners during the blitz of 1940. For the Israelis, as for the British during that year when they fought on alone against the Axis powers, there was no one to help them but themselves. In Israel, there was nowhere to retreat. For most of the people, there was nowhere else to go. The country had to fight to hold every field, every home.

Fortunately for Israel, the five invading Arab armies were never able to agree to a unified command or to a common strategy. In the beginning the Israelis, too, were torn by rivalries. The Haganah and the Palmach commandos were well disciplined and could be counted on. But anger at Arab guerrilla attacks before the end of the mandate, frustration at the blockade and the arms embargo, and impatience at the attempts of Ben-Gurion until the very last to come to terms with the Arabs and the British, led a number of hotter heads to break away from the Zionist authorities and band together in two terrorist gangs, Irgun and the Stern Group. Between them, they gave Ben-Gurion and the more responsible leaders almost as much trouble as the British. Sworn to terrorize the British into quitting the country, the gangs bombed police headquarters and government offices, assassinated officials and kidnapped and murdered British soldiers, booby-trapping the bodies. They took credit not only for the blowing up of the King David Hotel and the killing of the head of the Swedish Red Cross, the United Nations Mediator in Palestine, Count Folke Bernadotte, but also for the massacre of two hundred men, women and children in an Arab village named Dir Yassin believed to have been harboring Arab snipers. The terrorists brought some of the bodies of the villagers back to Jerusalem with them to prove their deed. In defiance of the Israeli government which had agreed to a United Nations cease-fire, they later brought a ship named the *Altalena* to Tel Aviv with arms and ammunition for the Irgun. After the Irgun refused to heed the warning that their action constituted sabotage and treason, Ben-Gurion was finally forced to give the order to blow up the ship. Twelve people were killed, and there was a pitched battle in which Jew fought Jew. But the Israeli government had made clear its authority.

Public opinion had turned against the savagery of the terrorists. They were discredited and disarmed. There was a thorough reorganization of the Israeli Army aimed at eliminating divisive tendencies. Younger men were given command posts. The archeologist Yigael Yadin, then thirty-two, was appointed Chief of Operations. Moshe Dayan, a thirty-three-year-old lieutenant colonel, was the commander of Jerusalem under siege.

Jerusalem was hit harder by the enemy than any other part of the country. Heavily shelled by the Jordanian Arab Legion under British officers, the hundred thousand Jewish inhabitants were isolated for five months until Israeli forces could punch a new route through the surrounding Arab territory to relieve them. On what is now the main road to Jerusalem, a few of the burnt-out wrecks of cars from the convoys that made the trip are left as memorials beside the road as it winds through the woods and hills up to Jerusalem.

During Israel's War of Independence, Ben-Gurion as Commander-in-Chief drew on Joshua's Biblical campaigns against the Canaanites, on the Maccabees' guerrilla techniques, and on the lessons of the wars between Athens and Sparta. Everything had to be improvised, in a hurry and while under fire. Haifa was taken more or less by loudspeaker, and Safed by a homemade mortar called Little David which made a tremendous bang and was credited with convincing the enemy there that the Jews had an atom bomb.

"Davidka" mortar

In the middle of this war, the Government of Israel had not only to put an army into the field and to create and equip an air force and navy, but also to build camps for tens of thousands of immigrants, to design postage stamps and coins, write the law of the land and enforce it, create a foreign service, immigration, customs, police, fire and sanitation departments. Arms and ammunition had to be manufactured. All this had to be done simultaneously, and, David Catarivas, Israeli diplomat and author, has reported, "a top hat found for the Marshall of the Diplomatic Corps."

The day after the mandate ended, Israel opened its doors to immigration. Any Jew in the world was welcome, and conditions were wretched enough, or so dangerous, for the Jewish communities in other parts of the world that—even in the middle of an invasion with the infant nation fighting for its life—five thousand refugees arrived in the first two weeks. Many of them learned to handle a rifle before they learned

Hebrew (some of the difficulties experienced by this polygot army were a factor in the great emphasis given ever since to the immigrants' rapid learning of their new national language).

Jewish and non-Jewish recruits and volunteers arrived from overseas. The stream of refugees became a torrent.

The first months of the State of Israel saw violent warfare punctuated by a series of truces enforced by the United Nations, deeply concerned lest this spark in the Middle East set off a Third World War.

In the intervals between truces, the Israeli forces, improvisation and all, were more than a match for their opponents. Remembering the scourges loosed against the Pharaoh by Moses, the Israelis named Operation Ten Plagues their lightning attack against the Egyptians begun in the south on October 15, 1948. Within one week, the Israel Defense Forces had sunk several Egyptian ships including the flagship *King Farouk,* destroyed a fair number of planes on the ground and great stores of fuel and other military supplies. Beersheba, the most important Egyptian base in the Negev, was taken on October 22. The other Arab forces made no attempt to come to the rescue of the Egyptians.

The following month, in Operation Lot, the Israelis secured strong points which gave them control over the route to Sodom at the southern end of the Dead Sea, and strengthened Israeli control of their share of the Negev. By March 10, 1949, after a dash through the desert and the jagged mountain wasteland of the Negev that took the enemy completely by surprise, an armored column raised the flag of Israel over a small shack on the shores of the Gulf of Aqaba, giving Israel possession of territory which it had been assigned under the partition proposals of the United Nations. This breakthrough, affording Israel access to the Red Sea and a way to the countries of Africa and Asia that lay beyond the Arab states, was an incalculable political, economic and military advantage.

An unexpected turn of events helped the State of Israel secure itself during the first precarious days, yet was to create a grave problem for the future. This was the decision of the Arab states to call on Arabs living in Israel to evacuate the country and thus ease the advance of the invading Arab armies. The Arab radio alarmed its listeners with tales of Jewish atrocities in Israel, and warned that it would be impossible for the invading forces, bent on vengeance, to distinguish between Jew and Arab. Most of the Arabs in Israel, including almost all of their religious and civic leaders, fled to the side of the Arab states.

In many places, there were efforts until the last to enable the Jews and Arabs to work together. In a few, where the local

A girl watches the frontier

Arab leaders refused to budge, the Arab communities remained where they were, and managed to ride out the storm. The Israeli government attempted to stay the panic. In Haifa, with sixty-two thousand Jews and sixty-two thousand Arabs, the Mayor, Shabtai Levy, wept as he asked the Arabs to stay. An Arab delegation of two Moslems and four Christians replied that they must get in touch with the Arab states, and later that day returned to say they must leave. The British Major General Stockwell presiding at the meeting (just before the end of the mandate) was openly shocked. British residents of Haifa and Jewish neighbors begged the Arabs not to leave. But all but five or six thousand fled, following the departure of their leaders, in the face of threatening Arab broadcasts.

At the same time, it must be recognized that there were deliberate Jewish attacks on some Arab settlements whose positions were considered strategically vital, like those on Lod and Ramla, on the way to Jerusalem.

Departure of most of the Arab population greatly simplified the security problems of the Israeli government and made easier the work of its defense forces. Conversely, the pellmell flight of more than six hundred thousand Arab civilians got in the way of the advance of thirty thousand Arab troops. Those in charge of invasion plans, who had promised the refugees temporary haven, then a return with the victorious troops to a Palestine for Arabs, now found themselves burdened with the homeless population.

The saddest thing about all of this, it seems to me, is that it need not have happened. In spite of the preaching of hostility between the communities and the increasing bitterness and violence in the closing years of the mandate, there are obviously many—perhaps an increasing number—on both sides who would be willing to live and let live. An outsider who travels from one side to the other as a pilgrim or a tourist, discovers an almost wistful desire to hear how things look in enemy territory,

A view of Old Jerusalem

an eagerness to believe there are many among the enemy who would like peace. Twice in the Old City of Jerusalem my wife and I have had Palestinian refugees who became Jordanians, wish us a good-natured *"Shalom!"* in Hebrew instead of *"Salaam!"* in Arabic when they realized we must have arrived from the other side with the thousands of pilgrims who come every Christmas and Easter. A guide to the holy places told us how life used to be in Jaffa where he lived when he worked as a radio operator at Tel Aviv's Lydda airport. He sounded sad.

114

The war between Israel and its Arab neighbors came to an end in 1949 when talks were held on the Greek island of Rhodes and armistice agreements were signed by most of the belligerents (Iraq and Saudi Arabia refused). With the help of Dr. Ralph Bunche, the American political scientist who had succeeded the slain Count Folke Bernadotte as United Nations Mediator, relations between the Israelis and their Arab antagonists were relatively cordial. But they had chilled by the time a conciliation commission met at Lausanne in Switzerland to draft the final peace treaties. This the Arab countries now refused to do, and throughout five months of meetings with the United Nations Mediator, the two delegations did not meet, officially, face to face. One of the ironies of the conference was that the delegation of Palestinian refugees—who had lost most of all in the war, for they had lost their country—were avoided by the Egyptian delegation. The refugee Arabs spoke mainly to the Jewish Israelis.

At Lausanne, as part of a general settlement, Israel offered to admit immediately a hundred thousand refugees, to reunite separated families, and to pay compensation for abandoned lands. These terms were rejected by the Arab side. The conference ended with the uneasy armistice still in effect, but no treaty of peace. One by one, however, almost all the nations except the Arab states recognized Israel, and on May 11, 1949, Israel was admitted as the fifty-ninth member of the United Nations.

Officially, the war was over. But peace was still far away. Skirmishes along the frontiers became more and more frequent. There were raids and counterraids across the border. Commando teams of fedayin were trained and sent into Israel from Egypt and Syria as guerrilla raiders. In retaliation Israeli commandos destroyed several of the fedayin bases just across the border. The tempo of frontier sabotage, assassination, am-

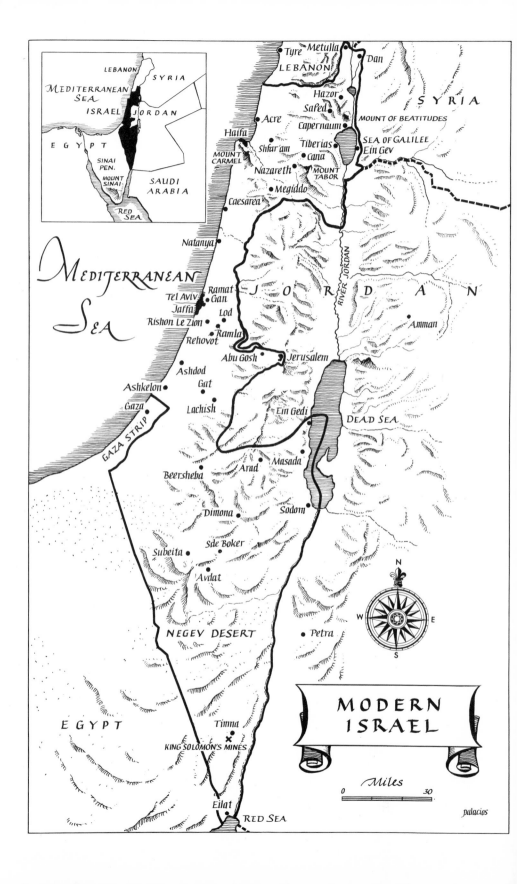

MODERN
ISRAEL

bush and espionage increased. In the first eight years Israel lost nearly fourteen hundred frontier settlers to the hit-and-run raids of the fedayin who were becoming increasingly successful and professional terrorists. At the same time, the Arab states openly discussed the chances in a second round in a war of extermination against Israel, and built up large stocks of arms, mostly from the Soviet bloc.

All of this was given by the Israel government as justification for its six-day Operation Sinai which began on October 29, 1956. It can be described either as a police action or an invasion, depending on the side one takes. In any case, it lasted less than a week and ended with the capture by the Israelis of five thousand prisoners (soon released), and of vehicles, artillery and other weapons, ammunition, fuel and medical supplies in quantities unknown before to the Egyptian forces.

Coordinated with Operation Sinai was the Anglo-French Suez invasion, an old-fashioned exercise in gunboat diplomacy which failed dismally in its objective: to regain and hold the Suez Canal. Egypt had just seized the canal from the Anglo-French organization which had built it and had been intended to run it until 1968. In the end, and with United Nations members from the United States to the Soviet Union objecting that this was a dangerous way to settle a dispute, Egyptian authority was restored in Suez. French and British forces were withdrawn, and Israeli troops pulled back from Sinai and Gaza. But Israel had proven itself in combat against superior numbers and equipment and had broken up the major fedayin bases.

Since the Sinai Operation, life in Israel has been relatively quiet. This and the War of Independence are still a part of the lives of most people in the country . . . just as one is always aware of the fifty thousand Israeli survivors of the Nazi camps. But life goes on. In Israel, in place of uncertain exile and possible death is greater security, a decent present, and a future

Atomic Reactor

that—in the eyes of the pioneers—is glowing. The severe
rationing of the war years is ended. The Hula swamp has been
drained. Pipelines are laid. One atomic reactor has been put
into operation, and another is being built. The merchant
shipping between Israel and Africa and the Far East increases
by twenty per cent a year. It is just possible that their enemies
could indeed erase Israel from the map and exterminate or
send once again into exile all those who have returned to their
ancient homeland. But it would seem that the Israelis are home
to stay.

Chapter 9

AMERICAN COUSINS

Both the United States and the State of Israel are countries created by immigration. Both were settled first by the pioneers—idealists and trail blazers—then by "an ever-growing stream of refugees from other countries."

The American association with the Zionist dream is an old and honorable one. In 1818, some forty years before Theodor Herzl was born, the second president of the United States, John Adams, wrote, "I really wish the Jews again in Judea, an independent nation . . ." He was writing to Major Mordecai Manuel Noah, the son of a sergeant in George Washington's army, who as American Consul in Tunis six years before had become famous for liberating the crews of several American ships from the Barbary pirates who infested the North African coast. Major Noah became fascinated with the idea of re-creating the Jewish nation in its homeland, and in 1825, with the support of President Adams, laid the cornerstone of a "City of Refuge" on Grand Island in the Niagara River. There land was cleared, and Jewish refugees from Europe were to be given agricultural training and prepared for life in Palestine. The response of European Jewry was disappointing. No one now knows how many came to the City of Refuge. All that is left is the cornerstone, preserved by the Buffalo Historical Society. Major Noah was far ahead of his time. But it seems that he, an

American Jew, was the first in modern times to dream and make practical plans for the return to Zion. And it was an American President who became the first head of state to express his sympathy with this dream.

American interest in Palestine continued to grow, and in 1844 the State Department appointed Warder Cresson as United States Consul to the Turkish Court for "All the Holy Land." Within a year of establishing residence in Jerusalem, Mr. Cresson became converted to Judaism and changed his name to Michael Boaz Israel. A dreamer, certainly, and denounced to the Secretary of State as a lunatic, the new Mr. Israel nevertheless persisted and in 1847 founded outside Jerusalem a colony called "God's Vineyard." So far as we know now, this was the first modern Jewish agricultural colony. Drawing on his own experience as a farmer and with the Bible as his guide to farming in the Holy Land, Michael Boaz Israel in four years attracted two hundred American settlers, about a quarter of them Jews and the rest converts to Judaism, or Protestants who saw themselves also as ardent Zionists.

In 1871, the Holy Land Settlement Society was founded near Jaffa by a Polish-American farmer named Simon Berman, straight from the Wild West with cowboy boots and a six-shooter. By 1902, the number of Americans under the protection of the Jerusalem Consulate was over a thousand, and Selah Merill, Head of the Consulate, reported to Washington that, "had it not been for Turkish immigration restrictions, their number would have soared to eight or ten thousand assuredly . . ." ·

The Sultan of Turkey in 1882 forbade immigration of Jews into the Holy Land and all the rest of the province of Syria, though under the richly corrupt and incompetent Turkish colonial administration, many of the Jewish pilgrims simply melted into the landscape and remained as settlers.

This prohibition remained in force until the end of Turkish rule during the First World War. About the same time, after the assassination in 1881 of the Russian Czar Alexander II and the charging by the Russian government of the Jews as a scapegoat, there was a wave of pogroms throughout Eastern Europe. Fleeing persecution and mob violence, Eastern European Jews found one door open to them, Emma Lazarus' "golden door," as she wrote in the poem on the base of the Statue of Liberty after watching the unending stream of destitute Eastern European Jewry. Two and a half million Jewish refugees reached the United States in the next three decades.

American immigration policy was liberal, and until 1907 citizenship was easily acquired. And naturalized Americans were not penalized for living outside the United States. With special consideration being given American Jewish citizens in the Holy Land by the Turkish government who were anxious to please the United States, there was a good deal of inter-migration. Many Eastern European families emigrating in the nineteenth century went partly to Palestine, partly to the United States. A sense of kinship, close family feeling between relatives on both sides, survives to this day.

Some ten thousand Americans came to settle as pioneers in Israel before its independence. A few thousand more came as religious scholars to Jerusalem. Then there were the two thousand American volunteers for the Jewish Legion in the First World War, and the seventeen hundred American veterans who joined the Israel defense forces in 1947.

In the tradition of Major Noah and Michael Boaz Israel, remarkable Americans continued to crop up with fair regularity. One of the most remarkable was Henrietta Szold, an American spinster who must have been possessed of great practicality and overwhelming warmth and compassion to accomplish all that she did. Henrietta Szold in 1912 founded

Hadassah, the American Women's Zionist organization which a year later sent two nurses and three doctors to Jerusalem. Still later when America was at war with Turkey's ally Germany, though precariously neutral toward Turkey herself, the Hadassah medical team somehow continued to operate. In Palestine there was typhus, cholera, and starvation. P. E. Lapide, the Canadian-Israeli chronicler of the American and Canadian migration, has written: ". . . self-appointed Pimpernels bullied, bribed and threatened Turkish officials into more humane attitudes." American medical supplies were smuggled into Palestine, and in the end, the American Navy evacuated the aged and disabled. This helping hand from the United States, which was at war with the local authorities, may well have saved from disintegration and yet another dispersal, the dwindling Jewish colony in Palestine.

Six months before the end of the First World War, forty-four nurses and doctors calling themselves the American Zionist Medical Unit arrived in Palestine to carry on and do what they could until the British medical authorities could take over. More than half the volunteers remained to plan Hadassah hospitals and clinics, set up the working man's ubiquitous Histadrut Sick Fund.

Henrietta Szold

Children arriving in Israel from Iraq

Not content with founding Hadassah—a far-ranging program of medical research, preventive and curative medicine, public health and hygiene services, a school lunch program and a social welfare department—Henrietta Szold in 1920 also worked with Israel's WIZO (Women's International Zionist Organization) to help take care of children and immigrant expectant mothers. Then, from 1933 until her death twelve years later at the age of eighty-five, she directed Youth Aliya, responsible for rescuing children from the Nazi terror and getting them to Palestine. Britons and Americans and those in relatively safe parts of the world who wanted to settle in Palestine were asked to wait, or if they felt they had to come, to come illegally, so that their precious places in the immigration quota could be used to save more children.

Youth Aliya brought more than a hundred thousand children to Israel in its first thirty years, orphans who came to youth villages and schools and agricultural settlements in Israel, children who came as an advance guard for their families. It is the extraordinary achievement of an extraordinary woman.

"Five wars, two naval blockades, a host of prohibitions and barricades and one long, uneasy truce," writes Lapide, "—none of these could ever stop American Jews, not even for a single year, from making their way to the Land of Israel."

There were Americans among those who came to help run the blockade, bringing refugees to Israel in the postwar years. More came to join the Israelis in the War of Independence. Now, five hundred to a thousand come to Israel as immigrants each year; there are perhaps altogether ten thousand Israelis of American nationality, and the inevitable crop of jokes about their building completely air-conditioned pioneer kibbutzim. Another seventy-five thousand American tourists, about two-thirds of them Jewish, visit Israel annually.

Of the Jewish Americans among the visitors, many have

Beach at Tel Aviv

relatives in the country. Some come for a season each year; others come to retire. What they find is a far cry from the austerity of the first years of independence. The days of rationing are far behind. When the athletes came to Israel for the first Maccabeean games they had to be put up in tents. There are now strings of hotels along the sandy bluffs of Tel Aviv, looking out over the ships riding at anchor in the Mediterranean. Tourist oases have sprung up in the desert of the Negev. The kibbutzniks have built swimming pools. And fashions—though they suffer something of a sea change—take few weeks to make their way from New York to Israel.

There has also grown up in the United States a group of non-Jewish Israel enthusiasts. They range from mink ranchers to distinguished anthropologists and physicists, people who are impressed with the progress Israel is making, and who have caught something of the pioneering spark. They teach or lecture in their specialties, help new enterprises to get started, or observe and return to report to Americans at home what they have seen. Brigadier General S. L. A. Marshall, known as Slam, editorial writer and military editor of the *Detroit News,* who has kept abreast of developments in Israel since he covered the fighting during the War of Independence, makes it a point to return to the country every year or so. My old friend and mentor Karl Schmidt, the Curator-in-Chief of Zoology at the Chicago Natural History Museum and a man who had worked in many parts of the world, made it a point, until his death recently, to return to teach in Israel because he felt that in few places in the world did people accomplish so much with what little they had. Dr. Schmidt was particularly struck with the way small communities as well as the larger towns often had their own well-ordered zoos or museums, each drawing on whatever was available in that locality, helping to teach the people there something about the world they lived in.

It is hard to remember, with the tempo of construction and the obvious faith in the future, that the country still lives under a sort of siege, and that the shooting war was recent and is still very near. Then, there is suddenly a reminder: the tangle of barbed wire in the sand under the hotel's picture windows giving out over the sea; the eyeless windows of a bombed-out house next to a modern agricultural school in the Jerusalem Corridor. Behind a weathered wooden fence on a main street of Tel Aviv is a ruined building and gaping hole like a bomb site in London after the blitz.

The policemen's uniforms remain smartly British, as does the judicial system and the accent of many of the announcers of Kol Israel's excellent English newscasts, though there is one breezy, resolutely American disk jockey named Yehuda Lev who can turn out the most enthusiastic St. Patrick's Day program this side of New York. But there is surprisingly little in Israel that seems specifically British. Rather than drive on the left, as do the British, people here drive on the right, just as they did all through the mandate. There is a marked enthusiasm for things American, from authors to chewing gum to anything made of plastic. There is Israeli interest in American techniques in everything from surgery to hotel management.

In many fields, the curiosity and willingness of the American and the Israeli to learn from each other is reciprocal.

Glass pavilion of the Museum Haaretz, Tel Aviv

Chapter 10

THE TOURIST

Except for the raw winter months most of the year Israel seems to be host to special buses, cars and trains filled with tourists, hikers, hitchhikers and loners who refuse to go in groups. They visit the museums and the galleries, go to live at the kibbutzim and join Israeli archeological expeditions.

There are a remarkable number of museums and collections of all kinds to be seen in this small country. Museums house modern art and Japanese art and Jewish folklore, Roman

127

mosaics, Christian relics, Islamic art and collections of archeological interest.

In the kibbutzim, American boys and girls and visitors from
other countries work in the fields with the kibbutzniks. They
join Hebrew University's archeological expeditions in the caves
around the Dead Sea, serving as volunteers in the infinitely
painstaking search for records of the ancient Hebrew civiliza-
tions, and tools and vessels left by the prehistoric cave dwellers.
The most exciting archeological treasures of 1961 were dis-

Israeli motor cycle policeman and a Bedouin in the Negev

covered by a girl on vacation from her university in Argentina.

Visitors like to go south to Beersheba—a city of modern functional buildings with expanses of glass and brightly-colored vertical louvers that act as sun-breaks—rising in the desert beside the ancient town. Trains of camels and mules laden for the Monday and Thursday markets follow the highway and the telephone lines into town. Government Tourist Corporation notes for visitors remind them that in the market in Beersheba they can buy a baby camel "to surprise your friends"; and on market mornings, the health service clinics do a brisk business with the Bedouins, come to town from all over the Negev.

At Beersheba one can also inspect a rather decrepit hole known as Abraham's Well, see the camel market and the Bedouin women with their faces half hidden by festoons of silver coins, visit the gleaming new hospital buildings, the starkly handsome modern synagogue and the community center.

Most of the travelers are old enough to have the time and a little money to go abroad. But, increasingly, there are younger teachers and students touring Israel, teenagers with rucksacks on the road or in the youth hostels scattered over the country. There was nothing remarkable in the fact that late one afternoon at a filling station in the middle of the desert, my wife and I picked up three young Americans, two girls and a boy, from Hebrew University in Jerusalem (the Americans are the largest foreign contingent there), bound for Eilat where they planned to sleep thriftily on the beach.

At Eilat visitors ride in glass-bottomed boats over coral beds somewhat depleted by souvenir manufacturers. They peer at the awkwardly stuffed fish in the Red Sea Maritime Museum. They listen to Israeli songs around campfires on the beach. Above all, they catch something of the vitality of this frontier town, at the end of Israel, where wages are high and so are prices, and where construction is even more frenetic than in other parts of the country. Where there was little more than a shack a few years ago, there is now a town of ten thousand, and a port busy with tankers from the Persian Gulf with oil for the pipeline to Haifa, with the African- and Israeli-manned ships carrying passengers and cargo to Ethiopia and Madagascar, India, Hong Kong and Japan. Hotels are springing up, and there are night clubs hung with fishermen's floats and nets, run by bearded characters, and with names like "The Blue Dolphin" and "The End of the World."

The tourists go north from Tel Aviv in the black touring cars with the emblem of grapes on their sides, or in fleets of buses. Mark Twain wrote in *The Innocents Abroad* of how disappointed he was during his visit to the Holy Land to find grapes scarcely the size of those in his childhood picture books, which looked to be "a respectable load for a pack train." He also lamented the lack of a railroad, for travel through the Holy Land by horse was arduous enough to give an idea of the

New housing at Eilat

Biblical trek of seven days from Dan to Beersheba, and to help
explain why Israel and the neighboring kingdoms in the Bible
—with the concentration of a thousand years and more of
history and tradition, and long familiarity with so many of the
characters—seem unexpectedly small when visited. Mark
Twain comments that the "combined monarchies of the thirty
'kings' destroyed by Joshua on one of his campaigns, only
covered an area about equal to three or four counties of
ordinary size." But so it must be, when the visitor bumps into
history—often his own—every few feet.

Not far from Tel Aviv and Jaffa on the way north is Megiddo,
the scene of the Biblical battle of Armageddon which, it is fore-
told, will signal the end of the world. Scholars have suggested
that Megiddo was chosen since it had been the site of battles
and invasions as long as the memory of man; now, it is fertile,
peaceful, quiet country.

Roman statue at Ashkelon

Along the coast between Jaffa and Haifa, with its sand dunes carefully planted in an agricultural experiment (successful but costly), and with the waterbirds wading in the ponds beside the track that follows the shoreline, the finned, black tourist cars pull off the highway that follows the same route, and stop while their passengers photograph the imposing, broken walls of Herod's port of Caesarea, the colossal, heroic Roman statues, and the Caesarea Golf Club—Israel's one and only links—across the way.

Driving north and east from the coast, the cars and the tourist buses press on to Nazareth. Here, in the steep and narrow cobbled streets, with guides herding pilgrims from one sacred spot to another, and hawkers running alongside offering rosaries and crying, "Arab headdress! Arab headdress!", there is the odd mixture of the holy and the commercial which seems to exist in centers of pilgrimage. Nazareth is now an Arab town of twenty-five thousand against Tel Aviv's four hundred thousand, Haifa's hundred and eighty thousand and Israeli Jerusalem's hundred and sixty-five thousand. It is a poor town, with jobs relatively scarce in this land of full employment, and a fairly large work force traveling each day to Haifa. After Jerusalem and Bethlehem, Nazareth is the goal of Christian pilgrims because of its association with the New Testament's description of thirty years of the life of Christ. Here is the Church of the Annunciation and its grotto where, it is believed, the Virgin Mary was told of the coming birth of Christ by the Archangel Gabriel. Here are the caves where the early Christians lived; the Church of St. Joseph; the pilgrims' hostels and the schools and orphanages and hospitals and clinics of all the Christian orders which have come to Nazareth.

Nazareth with the Franciscan Monastery and the Church of St. Joseph in the foreground

Jerusalem remains the holy of holies. For Moslems, it is the place where Mohammed touched down on his night flight to Paradise on his marvelous steed, Al Buraq, and the site of the gilded Mosque of the Dome of the Rock on Mount Moriah. There, Abraham, common ancestor of Jews, Christians and Moslems, offered to sacrifice his son Isaac, as told in the Book of Genesis. For Jews, it is the city of Mount Zion and its Tomb of David where in a rocky niche candles flicker in his memory. Where the Mosque now stands in the Old City was the First Temple built by David's son Solomon, then the Second Temple, rebuilt by Herod the Great with ten thousand workmen and a thousand priests who became masons in order to build the holiest parts of the great building which only they could enter. Barred from the Mosque itself, the Jews

Jewish elders meditating

Mt. Zion and the Valley of Gei-Hinnom (the Biblical Hell) in Jerusalem

for centuries came to lament their destruction at the Wailing
Wall, now a part of the Mosque's exterior, and the only substantial part surviving of the Herodian temple. Since the division of the city, Jews have—most painfully—been cut off from
this remainder of the Temple.

For Christians, Jerusalem is the scene of the last days of
Christ, of his Crucifixion, and of the Church of the Holy Sepulchre which stands at the site of the Crucifixion. Here are the
sites of the Garden of Gethsemane where Christ was betrayed,

the Mount of Olives where Christ ascended to Heaven, the room where Christ and the Disciples took the Last Supper, the Church of the Dormition on the spot where the Virgin Mary died. There are priests and nuns in the robes of the orders in charge of these and the multitude of Christian holy places, in both Israeli and Jordanian Jerusalem. Most of them, including the Church of the Holy Sepulchre, are in Jordan. Thousands of Christians—including tourists with cameras and African students in voluminous, brightly colored cottons—each year make their way from the Israeli side of Jerusalem through the tank traps of that sad, battered passageway known as the Mandelbaum Gate to take part in the Christmas and Easter celebrations.

It is like going to the moon. On the other side of the Old City's great wall built by Suleiman the Magnificent, are crooked narrow streets with the arches overhead and small dark stores with an occasional neon glare. The stores are crammed with cakes and candies, bolts of imported cloth, necklaces and vegetables, souvenirs and celluloid toys, comic books, daggers and brass trays, hubble bubbles, underwear and paperbound reprints of the classics. This is another world, so strongly a part of the Middle East that it might have been created by Hollywood. This is a bazaar, as it feels and looks and smells from here to China. Walking through the streets—shadows shot through with splashes of brilliant light—is like swimming through a school of fish. There are merchants and students, women with veils, small boys darting in and out, men of the Arab Legion in olive drab with the regulation strawberry-and-white figured headdress, secretaries from the American embassies in Amman and Tel Aviv, tiny, overloaded Biblical burros, more tourists with more cameras who have left their cruise ship in one country and who will rejoin it in another. Israel's New City with its dramatically modern university and hospital on its hills, its zealously orthodox community in beards and long coats, broad

Hebrew University

brimmed hats and all the trappings of medieval Jewish Europe, its outlying collective villages inhabited by refugees from India, Iran, Iraq and half the world—all this seems very far away as one stands a few hundred yards on the other side of the border in Jordan. And in many very real ways it is, too, for except for those getting special permits to cross over and back for the religious holidays twice a year, anyone who is not a diplomat and goes from Israeli Jerusalem to Jordanian Jerusalem and wishes to return must travel back via Cyprus.

137

It is a strange part of the world in which we live that countries can be divided into mutually hostile parts like the two Vietnams, the two Koreas, the two Chinas and the two Germanies, or great cities cut in two like Berlin and Jerusalem. In the two Jerusalems, there are separate power, water and sewerage systems. There is an airport, but it is in Jordan; there is a railway station, but it is in Israel. Yet one can hear the dogs bark at night on the other side of town, in another country. And the cannon fired at sunset each day in the Old City during the Moslem holy month of Ramadan is faithfully echoed in the kosher kitchens of the King David Hotel in Israel.

Travelers coming to Israel through the Mandelbaum Gate find themselves in a land where the rocky, dust-colored hills are beginning to sprout patches of green—saplings which Israel's National Fund urges visitors to come and help plant.

Visitors plant their trees, conscientiously inspect the hospitals and the nurseries, the kibbutzim and the schools. From Jerusalem to Eilat, it is hard to find an institution or a settlement that doesn't have a steady stream of visitors. On the walls of the dining rooms, in the dormitories, on the cornerstones, everywhere, are the thousands of plaques saluting the generosity of benefactors. Most of them are from the United States or Canada.

It is a dedicated and youthful minority among the American visitors who give their vacations to working with the Israelis on the land, to the exciting but tough work with the archeological expeditions in the caves among the cliffs around the Dead Sea. But there are very few of any age who come and see Israel who do not feel something of the excitement of the frontier, a part of America's own tradition.

A Habimah performance

Chapter 11

THE CULTURE OF THE COUNTRY

The meaning of the word "culture" is elusive. Many use the word, but most would be hard put to come up with a clear definition. Perhaps that given by the British anthropologist Edward Burnett Tylor nearly a century ago is as good a working description as any: "Culture is that complex whole which includes knowledge, belief, art, morals, law, custom and any other capabilities acquired by man as a member of society."

In Israel, culture, like almost everything else, begins with the Bible. Whatever else "culture" may mean, there is in this country an everlasting return to the Bible for inspiration and encouragement. "The Bible," says the Israel Government simply, "is the basis of Jewish nationhood, religion and culture." Bible study accounts for twenty to thirty per cent of the curricula of schools in Israel. These are the books of the Bible that the Christian world knows as the Old Testament. Christian, Moslem and Druze minorities in Israel share this common heritage, for the New Testament draws profoundly on the Old Testament, and both are sacred to Christianity. The Koran, the holy book of the Moslems, also derives inspiration from both Testaments. Just as Abraham is the father of the people of all three religions, so Christ is considered a major prophet in Islam, as are many of the Hebrew figures of the Old Testament.

In Israel, names are apt to be Biblical, from those of religious movements to those of sailors' bars along the waterfront ("Exodus" and "Garden of Eden"). Unconsciously, we use many Hebrew words and phrases in everyday English speech, from names like John and Mary to "Halleluiah!" and "seventh heaven." Israeli diplomats are encouraged to take Hebrew names, just as wives of Indians serving overseas are asked to wear saris. The exhaustive *Encyclopaedia Hebraica,* now appearing volume by volume, has forty thousand subscribers. There are more than seven hundred libraries in Israel (the United States, proportionately, would have sixty-three thousand instead of some fifteen thousand). During a walk in Tel Aviv down Allenby Road, a commercial artery not especially noted for arts or scholarship, one can count one hundred and twelve booksellers. Israel publishes more books per capita than any country outside Scandinavia.

Theater in Israel is a bit of everything. There are a couple of hundred amateur groups, there are pageants, army theatrical companies and troupes playing the kibbutzim and settlements of new Israelis—in Hebrew, Yiddish, Polish, Russian, English, Spanish, French and a half dozen other languages. Foreign companies from the Polish State Circus to a United States' Theater Guild troupe playing "The Glass Menagerie," "The Miracle Worker" and "The Skin of Our Teeth" all got a tremendous reception. There are three Israeli repertory companies, offering experimental drama and solid box office successes from Broadway, London and Paris. Among the popular imports have been "Saint Joan," "Cry the Beloved Country," "The Teahouse of the August Moon," "The Merchant of Venice," "Twelfth Night" and "The Diary of Anne Frank." Of the rep companies, Habimah, which gives five hundred performances a year, was founded in Russia in 1918, a year after the Revolution, moved to Israel ten years later, and thirty years after that, on Independence, was recognized as the Israel National Theater.

Far fewer Hebrew films are made than plays played, but movie attendance is high both in Israel and its neighbor Lebanon. Most movies are imported from the United States, France, Britain, Italy, Egypt, Spain and the Soviet Union, in about that order, with a scattering from other countries. Cus-

The Habimah Theater

tomarily, subtitles are run in Hebrew and in English or French, depending on which language the actor is speaking (if it is bilingual French-English dialogue, the subtitles hop back and forth). There is a not-unexpected demand for American or Italian films with Biblical themes. These are loosely based on the Bible, often with improbable plot and dialogue. Still, these *are* the stories and this *is* the place, and just the reminder that this is where it all happened can be an exciting thing to anyone here.

These are the evening's entertainment, and with books, music and sport, the recreation of the country. There are a few night clubs in the main centers, and a moderate number of bars, but coffee at a sidewalk café or a visit to the movies are the choice of most people. One curious contrast with the United States is that in Israel—where people drink relatively little— beer and brandy and such are available at all sorts of places like gas stations and candy stores, and whenever a shop is open, rather than being sold at certain hours and under a complex system of controls, as in a country where people drink more.

There is no television, but it is coming, and there are already shops selling television sets—prestige purchases which can be tuned in on neighboring countries.

Music and dance are nourished by two mainstreams, each with many tributaries: the folk themes of Israel itself and the Middle East, and the many lands from which the Jews of the ingathering have come. There is the great classical legacy of Europe. The national dance is the hora, a driving, rhythmical folk dance originally from the Balkans. It is usually performed in a circle, punctuated with claps and shouts of *Hora! Hora!*, and has a close affinity to our own square dances. The first time I saw the hora danced was on the French Line ship *Libérté* in 1950, performed with infectious enthusiasm by a group of Jewish American students investing their vacations and their savings traveling tourist class to spend the summer working in

A group of young immigrants from Europe dance the hora

the kibbutzim of the State of Israel, born two years earlier. It is the dance now of the kibbutzniks, the visitors, and of most of Israel, of the "evenings of national song and dance and Israel folklore" and the holidays when the Government Tourist Corporation announces that "there will be merrymaking and dancing in the streets." There is something a little forced and savoring of the hothouse about all this, perhaps, as the new nation-state seeks its own personality. If the hora now, to an outsider, seems to lack the deep roots and distinctive flavor of the folk dances, say, of Mexico or India, or many other countries, these, too, should come in time.

Also a great feature of entertainment are the groups—usually amateur or semi-professional—of Israeli folk dancers who originally came from Eastern Europe and Soviet Central Asia. Most of them, with the exception of the Druzes, and of the Yemenites who have a rich and colorful tradition of their own, seem ever-fainter carbon copies of the dancers in the countries of their origin. The government-sponsored Yemenite Inbal

143

"The Bride" in a presentation by the Inbal Dance Trou

troupe, a notably successful exponent of this ancient, comic and most appealing school, has toured the United States twice in recent years.

For the rest, there are scores of folk and ballet dance schools, and the beginnings of indigenous Israeli ballet and opera. The music does not compare with European classical music, for which Israel provides one of the most appreciative audiences to be found—perhaps the most so. The Israel Philharmonic Orchestra has twenty-five thousand subscribers, which is, proportionately, the most enthusiastic support given any symphony orchestra anywhere. Many of its hundred and two members were under fire as the orchestra traveled under military escort during the War of Independence, but it never missed a performance. It now plays in the three-thousand-seat Frederic Mann auditorium in Tel Aviv, travels throughout the country and abroad, and attracts an array of soloists and guest conductors each year which would be an impressive catch for any of the great capitals. There is also the Kol Israel Orchestra, orchestras for the defense forces, the larger municipalities and the collective settlements. There are music festivals each year in the Roman amphitheater at Caesarea, and at Ein Gev, a fishing kibbutz on the far bank of the Sea of Galilee. There is an Israel Composers' Association whose two hundred members create concertos and cantatas, serious atonal efforts, and pop music ranging from the "Beer Barrel Polka" sort of Central European gallop to traditional Yiddish songs that always sound a little sad, even when they are not and, perhaps because they are written in a minor key, ring with overtones of the ghettoes of Eastern Europe. And, as always, there is cross-fertilization. The Arab music one hears over Kol Israel is like that coming over the air from the neighboring Arab states, and has many similarities to the music of Pakistan and India. And my wife Bertie and I have heard the American Yiddish favorite "Bei

The Yemenite Inbal Dance Troupe

Mir Bist Du Schön" being played over Radio Jordan, whose announcer was under the impression it was "an old German folk tune."

These many streams nourish the polyglot broadcasts and books and publications. There is an audience for theater and films in many languages, and an appreciation of good work from as many countries. Certainly, the standard of writing and editing in English is high, both in the press and on the radio. Kol Israel's broadcasters strike me as quicker to understand and interpret the significance of international news, and generally better than either those of the British Broadcasting Corporation or the Voice of America—which is curious since the latter are both working in their own language.

Israeli architecture is modern international in form and with a few notable exceptions, drab in style. A new mutual aid

A music festival in the ancient amphitheater at Caesarea

A torch bearer during the four-day march to Jerusalem

agreement with Brazil now calls for Israeli technical assistance in helping solve some of the problems of Brazil's drought-ridden, poverty-stricken northeastern bulge, while Brazil is to bring architectural guidance to Israel; remembering the brilliant work in modern tropical architecture done in Brazil over the past couple of decades, it will be interesting to see what happens in Israel in the next two.

Except for women's knitwear, which has captured a respectable international market, textiles and clothing in Israel are without distinction. The same must be said of the food, which is cosmopolitan, but can hardly be hailed as the best of the lands from which it comes, nor is it yet a truly interesting cuisine of its own. This is only to say that the Israeli national genius, like the British and the American, for the most part does not express itself in cooking.

Sport in Israel is of the usual, international variety, with an almost Scandinavian emphasis on hiking, culminating every year in a four-day march to Jerusalem to celebrate the annual custom of ancient Israelites from all the land of bringing offerings to the Temple. Now, indestructible types in their seventies

147

and eighties, scouts, delegations of African students, contingents from the athletic teams and businesses and collective settlements make the ascent to Jerusalem before Passover. There are the usual organized sports of most sorts, but no great specialization, no Israeli teams to compete with Americans in track, Russians in weight-lifting and gymnastics or Australians in swimming. Rather, camping and hiking and keeping fit for the pioneer life are emphasized.

Science, too, is international in character and not markedly different in Israel than that of other countries which are technologically advanced. But, here again, in the tradition of Chaim Weizmann, standards are high, and Israel has been able to attract outstanding scientists, researchers and technicians from around the world. There is particular interest in chemistry, computers, tropical medicine, agriculture, hydraulic engineering, solar energy, desalinization, irrigation and other problems of arid lands.

Israeli literature and writing in general find themselves in a time of transition. Yiddish, which is one of the world's great literary languages, is gradually giving way to Hebrew, and modern literary Hebrew is still trying its wings. The talent is here, the tradition is here, the audience is here, and it remains to see what will happen. It could be great.

In Israel one is continually brought back to the Bible. There is a constant underscoring of the spiritual base on which rests the country's culture. Abba Eban, Israel's Minister of Education and Culture, said at the dedication of Marc Chagall's stained glass windows at the synagogue of the Hadassah-Hebrew University Medical Center near Jerusalem, that Jerusalem had been enriched "by a new legacy of beauty and grace," going on to comment, "This city will never astound mankind by its wealth or physical power . . . Israel's place in history will be determined by her achievements in those realms where matter and quantity are transcended by mind and

Hebrew University synagogue

quality. Art, together with religion and science, is one of these worlds."

Chagall's windows represent the twelve tribes of Israel through their Biblical symbols (the Old Testament forbids, as does the Koran, the representation of the human form): Biblical birds and fish, the Lion of Judah, the Star of David, the seven-branched candelabrum, and the rest. Marc Chagall, a modern French artist born in the town of Vitebsk in eastern Russia, was a particularly happy choice. His use of luminous color has something of the quality—even on canvas—of sunlight through stained glass, and his painting has an evocative, other-worldly feeling. He said of his windows:

"How is it that the air and earth of Vitebsk, my birthplace, and of thousands of years of exile, find themselves mingled in the air and earth of Jerusalem?" This he asked at the dedication of his windows, speaking in Yiddish. "How could I have thought that not only my hands with their colors would direct me in my work, but that the poor hands of my parents and of others and still others with their mute lips and their closed eyes, who gathered and whispered behind me, would direct me . . . I feel, too, as though the tragic and heroic resistance movements in the ghettos, and your war here in this country, are blended in my flowers and beasts and my fiery colors.

One of Marc Chagall's stained glass windows

"These thoughts occurred to me many years ago, when I first set foot on Biblical soil to prepare to create etchings for the Bible," said Marc Chagall. "And they emboldened me to bring my modest gift to the Jewish people which always dreamt of Biblical love, of friendship and peace among all peoples . . . My hope is that I hereby extend my hand to seekers of culture, to poets and artists among the neighboring peoples . . . I saw the hills of Sodom and of the Negev, out of whose defiles appear the shadows of our prophets in their yellowish garments, the color of dry bread. I heard their ancient words . . . Have they not truly and justly shown in their words how to behave on this earth and by what ideal to live?"

Hebrew University lecture hall

Chapter 12

EDUCATION

To forge Israel again into one nation, school is a basic tool, and so, surprisingly, is the army.

From the ages of five to fourteen, education is compulsory, though some of the younger children, particularly among the Arab minorities and in the rural areas, manage to escape the net, if their parents are old-fashioned enough, poor enough and set enough in their ways to evade the authorities in order to keep their children home to help work on their farms. But even at the ages of three and four, a high proportion of the

152

children go to kindergarten; and running an accredited but free-lance kindergarten is a popular way for wives to augment the family income. Next door to us, in the other half of a double house, is such a kindergarten, alive with small fry wearing the national mushroom hats, chasing around the garden, sometimes being reprimanded, and generally having a good time. What is needed to start one's own kindergarten is a swing or two, perhaps a slide, a rubber tire brightly painted with furniture enamel, maybe a sandbox, a love of children, and meeting the kindergarten standards set by the government.

In Israel's elementary and high schools, there are now more than six hundred thousand students, as contrasted with about one hundred and thirty thousand at the time of Israel's independence. There are special classes for those between fourteen and eighteen who have not completed elementary school. A number of immigrants are illiterate. Hebrew becomes the first language in which they can read and write. There are a further ten thousand students at the university level.

In addition to religious seminaries, there are colleges serving students who will become teachers in the humanities, in law, science, agriculture and social work, and those who will specialize in medicine and public health and in trade union leadership. Others study chemistry, aeronautics, engineering, and architecture at the Technion in Haifa, which was founded in 1912 and is the oldest institution of higher learning in the country.

Most of the schools are coeducational, and tuition runs from the equivalent of about one hundred and forty to one hundred and ninety dollars a year. Students from families who cannot afford this may have up to eighty-five per cent of the cost paid by the Ministry of Education, and in exceptional cases, the complete tuition. The Ministry of Education and Culture also maintains more than three hundred clubs and playgrounds for school children and about a hundred youth centers, most of them in the pioneering regions being settled by the new Israelis. And there are fifteen youth hostels which are members of the World Association of Youth Hostels, with reciprocal privileges.

Hebrew is the language of instruction in most schools. Israelis soon find that modern Hebrew, whether they learn it in the first years of elementary school, in a crash language course for newcomers, or as part of their military service, is essential, binding them together as a people and as a nation.

Schools in the Arab areas use Arabic and teach Hebrew as a compulsory secondary language beginning with the fourth grade. Arabic is taught as an optional language in over a hundred schools. English is easily the most popular foreign language, though French is regaining something of its old international popularity, particularly with the emergence of the

Kfar Hayarok Agricultural School in the Sharon Valley

new French-speaking African nations, and is now taught in eighty-five schools in Israel.

In all of the schools, the curriculum is not unlike that of most American public schools, with the usual courses in mathematics and the other sciences, in history and literature, but with what would seem to us a remarkable emphasis on things Biblical. Even in "non-religious schools," the curriculum may be made up of nearly one-third Bible studies in one form or another. In the yeshivot, the hundred and seventy colleges, mostly in Jerusalem, which through the centuries have taught and interpreted the Hebrew Holy Scriptures, both civil and spiritual, there are now over nine thousand students.

Altogether, aside from the yeshivot, there are nearly twenty thousand students in some thirty institutions of higher learning in Israel. With the impetus the country now has, the numbers could easily change, as new schools and colleges are being opened at a steady rate.

Allied with the official, private and missionary efforts to provide education in Israel are a variety of youth movements. These include both Jewish and Arab Scouts; the Association of Working and School Youth, directly affiliated with the trade-union complex Histadrut; the Young Guard, associated with the left-of-center political party Mapam, and with close connections with the Arab Pioneering Youth Movement; the Pioneers' Camps of the Socialists; the Sons of Akiva, associated with the religious movement Hapoel Hamizrahi; the Young Maccabean, which specializes in sports, and is connected with similar Jewish Maccabi groups in other parts of the world; the Trumpeldor Alliance, closely related to the political party Herut; Zionist Youth, affiliated with the Liberals; and the Ezra movement, affiliated with the Religious Labor party. This close affinity of youth movements and political parties, like the trade unions, is closer to the European or Latin American tradition than to that of the United States or Canada.

The role of the military in education is of particular importance. (Even those people with the usual American antimilitary prejudice are impressed when they see what the Israeli army has done to help create a truly unified and democratic, self-reliant people.)

Military service is compulsory, with the exception of those young women from Orthodox families who choose for religious reasons not to serve and of a few young men whose nonmilitary work in medicine, teaching, engineering or agronomy is of special importance to the nation. Service is usually two and a half years for men, two years for women.

Gadna Youth Corps at Ramat Gan Stadium

All this begins with the Youth Corps, called Gadna, for boys and girls from fourteen to eighteen, in which they are given training that is a mixture of scouting, agriculture, archeological instruction, and the use of light arms. It is a common sight to see a dozen or so Gadna boys and girls in suntan shirts and slacks, ornamented with a variety of plastic water bottles, scarves and the familiar mushroom hats, hiking along one of Israel's highways or cutting cross-country as part of a lesson in camping out. There is Gadna training one day a week in all the high schools, and work on a farm or with the archeologists for a couple of weeks during the summer vacation. From the diggings, the Gadna students are allowed to take home bits of ancient pottery or other surplus not wanted by the museums, a dramatic and effective way of bringing to life the culture and the heritage of the new generation of Israelis. And, inevitably, the Gadna insignia is Biblical—the golden bow and arrow of King David against a diamond-shaped green background.

Particularly interested in both Gadna and in Nahal, the Pioneering Fighting Youth, are the students from some thirty-six other countries who now come to train in Israel. Nahal is one of the four national services which accepts only volunteers —the others are the paratroopers, pilots and submariners. It is composed of carefully selected groups of men and women who do their national service assigned to particularly exposed and dangerous frontier settlements. Nahal volunteers are given intensive military training, including commando courses; they may also study advanced agriculture.

My wife and I met many dozens of students and young servicemen and women, on their way to duty or on leave from the

A group on their way to a Gadna work camp at Lachish

Two Israeli parachutists

Israeli Air Force, Army or Navy, by giving them a lift in the car on our way to Tel Aviv or traveling about the country. Hitch-hiking is a part of the Israeli way of life, and it is common to stop and give hitchhikers a ride, especially those in uniform. Without a single exception those doing their military service have struck both of us as being immediately friendly, well-disciplined, and extremely polite. As a civilian with no military experience, I have been still struck by what is obviously the high professional quality, and the ease, yet decisiveness, of the young Israeli officers and non-commissioned officers.

Both the servicemen and the students are working to fulfill the educational goals of the country, which are high. An official government statement on education expresses the nation's attitude: "What Israel lacks in quantity she must make up in quality, and one of the most important factors in her progress is the extent to which the country can train scholars, professional men, scientists and technicians of high calibre."

Chapter 13

THE STATE, THE FUTURE

When I went to Israel, I asked CARE's acting chief of mission, Tony Matulewicz, what he thought was most important about the country. To him, it was a place of refuge for the Jews forced to flee other parts of the world. This was from a Roman Catholic, himself a second-generation Polish-American who had served in half a dozen countries, including Poland where the great prewar Jewish population had all but disappeared. By the time my wife and I had spent a couple of years in Israel, Tony's quick answer still seemed right.

To this should be added Jewish pride in the re-creation of the ancient homeland of a people who, at the same time, are among the most gifted, and among the most persecuted, group of human beings of whom the world has any record.

The nature of their new society reflects this. The two first facts of life for this new country are that it must be prepared to accept all those Jews in the world who want to return to Israel,

*An armed girl drives a tractor
on a kibbutz*

and that, in the face of hostile neighbors sworn to exterminate the state, it must somehow survive. The latter means that defense is of paramount importance; and this, unobtrusively, affects almost every aspect of Israeli national life. It is reflected in the high prices and the high taxes (much like ours in the United States), a large slice of which must go to keeping the country strong, and, one hopes, free. It is heard in the jet fighters which buzz the bluffs along the Mediterranean coastline (Mystères, Super-Mystères, and Mirages for Israel must rely on France for much of her arms). It is felt in the constant alert which the country keeps, even if the friendly tourists or Israelis going about their jobs are unaware of it most of the time. It can be seen in the groups of schoolboys and schoolgirls out hiking; sometimes they carry rifles. In schools, in books, in the press, in political speeches throughout the land, emphasis is placed not on those European ghetto dwellers who meekly

Kibbutz Ein Gev

accepted their fate, but on the ghetto resistance fighters in the Second World War, on the Maccabean nationalist handful who fought for Israel against the might of Imperial Rome. The frontier has been relatively quiet in the years since the Sinai campaign, but still the watchtowers are manned. Farmers plowing their fields near the borders are under fire, an occasional bus or truck on the lonely road through the desert to Eilat is attacked. The fishing kibbutz of Ein Gev on the Sea of Galilee, its fishermen out in their small boats and the police patrol launches have all been under sharp attack from Syria whose frontier nearby lies some forty feet from the water's edge. There is always the reminder that security is the first business of the state, or there will be no state.

Foreign policy is an important part of Israel's defense. The goal is establishment of friendly relations with the other countries of the Middle East, so that Israel may get on with the building of a new nation in its own diminutive, arid land. So it is that recognition of Israel by the newly independent island of Cyprus, like that of Turkey and Iran, in spite of pressure from the Arab states, is hailed in Israel as though it were a major victory in the Second World War. For Israel, it is. Israel now has diplomatic representation in most of the countries belonging to the United Nations, with the exception of the Arab states, and five others which the Israel government believes are particularly sensitive—often from what is seen as their own best national interest—to pressure by the Arab League. There are now nineteen Israeli embassies in Africa alone, and in most of these countries, Israeli doctors and engineers, teachers and agricultural experts are at work.

This policy, though costly, has been enormously beneficial to Israel. The results can be seen in the realization in these new nations and in many in Asia that Israel is not a tricky imperialist, but itself a small, underdeveloped country—even if one with remarkable resources, some money and a great deal of talent and determination—eager to share its experience with the African, Asian and Latin American countries facing similar problems. The results also show up in the votes in the United Nations, and in the increasing backing for the Israeli position that, to assure peace in the Middle East, the Arab states and Israel must meet and talk and resolve their differences. Israel's attitude has stimulated visits by African Moslem leaders who apparently feel no threat to their religion. And it is significant that the Prime Minister of Trinidad, just before the independence of his country, made Israel the objective of his first foreign visit, announcing on arrival that he had come because he hoped Israeli technicians might help with tackling problems in his home in the West Indies.

The Government of Israel trying to do all this is, in our meaning of the word, democratic. All authority rests in the legislature called the Knesset, a single chamber of one hundred and twenty representatives who are elected for four years. All adult Israelis may vote, and there are about a dozen political parties, ranging from middle-of-the-road to liberal, and including three Jewish religious parties of some power, three Arab parties representing various combinations of Moslems, Christians and Druzes, and a small Communist party. By one of those quirks that are the political facts of life, David Ben-Gurion's Mapai party, social-democratic, labor and basically secular in attitude, with far greater political strength than any of the others, remains in control of the present government only with the alliance of the religious parties, including the ultra-orthodox church-state supporters. Levi Eshkol succeeded Ben-Gurion as Prime Minister in 1963.

The Knesset elects the President for a five year term, and the President calls on the leader of the winning party in a national election to choose his Cabinet and form a new government. Cabinet members are usually Members of the Knesset, but are not required to be so, and sometimes are chosen from outside the legislature. Following the British parliamentary model, the government has only to lose a vote of confidence in the legislature, and a new parliamentary election must be called. The President's office is in great part ceremonial. As Chief of State, he signs all laws except those affecting his own office. He signs treaties approved by the Knesset, confirms Israel's diplomats, judges and the state's financial controller, and receives the stream, now mounting to a flood, of distinguished visitors from the Mediterranean, Asia, the Latin Americas, and above all, Africa who have come to see how Israel attacks the problems that they all share. The first President of Israel was Chaim Weizmann, fitting recognition of the man who had done so much to bring it into being. On Dr. Weizmann's death in 1952, Yitzchak Ben-Zvi was elected, re-elected in 1957 and served until his death in 1963. He was succeeded by Schneor Zalman Shazar.

A tall, spare, gently firm elder statesman and Biblical scholar, largely withdrawn from the infighting of politics, Ben-Zvi had been Ben-Gurion's fellow student in Istanbul when they were both learning Turkish law to help found a Jewish state within the Ottoman Empire. Then the two were roommates in cheap lodgings in New York, working for support of the Jewish cause in Palestine. Later both were labor organizers of Jewish and Arab farmers in Palestine during the days of the British mandate.

The government presided over by the President and directed by the Prime Minister and his Cabinet under the final authority of the Knesset is made up of Ministries of Agriculture, Commerce and Industry, Defense, Development, Education, Finance, Foreign Affairs, Health, Interior, Justice, Labor, Police, Posts, Religious Affairs, Social Welfare and Transport and Communications. The judiciary is independent.

Also of great importance in the life and daily business of the nation are the official Bank of Israel and the semi-official World

Menorah, the traditional Jewish candelabrum, in front of the Jerusalem Knesset

Zionist Organization and the Jewish Agency, which was mid-wife to the State of Israel, the United Israel Appeal which is the Agency's financial arm, and the Jewish National Fund which has been concerned with the acquisition of land (especially in pre-Israel Palestine), its reclamation, and the planting of more than sixty million trees in Israel's vast reforestation plan.

Under the British system of indirect rule, the Jewish Agency was the effective government of the Jewish community in Palestine. Now, with independence won, most of its authority has been transferred to the State of Israel, but the Jewish Agency still has an important role to play. It has brought to Israel over a million people from a hundred countries around the world and helped them to get started in its four hundred and eighty agricultural settlements, most of them founded since Israel's independence. Whatever the number, the state and its official and semi-official arms are sworn to take in the newcomers and to do their best to settle them all. The problem involves more than numbers. When the population of the state tripled shortly before independence, the number of blind grew ten times; with the ingathering of the survivors from Europe, the number of new citizens suffering from every sort of disability and needing special care, grew in like proportion.

Helping meet the needs are the voluntary organizations such as Hadassah with its Jerusalem hospital and medical school and network of clinics and mother and child health centers; the Israel Federation of WIZO (Women's International Zionist Organization) which maintains sixty-six youth clubs, and one hundred and twenty-one crèches, kindergartens and children's homes; Malben, which has established forty institutions to take care of the handicapped, the sick and the aged; Magen David Adom (the Red Shield of David), the Israel equivalent of the Red Cross; ORT, which for more than half a century has provided Jewish youth with vocational training. Like the Parsis of India and the Quakers of England and of the United States, Jews have placed great emphasis in investing a good share of their material gain in the welfare of the community.

As the only non-sectarian voluntary organization now in Israel, CARE shares in the support of these services with its program, begun in Europe at the end of the Second World War, through which friends and relatives could send packages of food to individuals. About seventy-five thousand of these specially-packed food parcels are still delivered in Israel each year. More important has been the use of American agricultural surplus—some twenty million pounds a year of milk powder, cottonseed oil, wheat flour, navy beans and corn meal—to help provide supplementary rations for institutions and for new immigrants. And there will be more immigrants, but when they will come is unpredictable. The hope, the dream in Israel is that one day Soviet Russia may permit not only the few who now come, but free immigration.

If this all sounds far removed, and a problem that can be solved without too much trouble, the illusion vanishes on visiting a newly arrived family. Those from North Africa may have half a dozen children, those from Europe fewer, and most of them find themselves beginning with nothing but hope in a new land. For the next few years, at least, there will be a great deal the voluntary agencies can do to help the new immigrants learn new skills, make a new life for themselves in their new home.

For those immigrants who learn a trade, the government, the trade unions and the voluntary organizations provide courses in metalworking, masonry, woodworking, electricity, mechanics and other skills needed to build a pioneer town in the wastes of the Negev. CARE supplies tool kits for the artisans and workshop equipment for a number of the schools where the newcomers are set on the road to making their own living. The investment is not wasted: every person trained supports himself and probably a family, becomes a productive member of the society, and helps to develop the frontier in the country of his adoption—much as did the settlers of the American West.

The cost of all this is enormous. It means some five hundred million dollars yearly in foreign investment, mostly from overseas Jewry, led by the South African, American and Canadian communities. The American connection remains particularly important, with U.S. social security benefits and pensions easily transferable to Israel for the considerable number who

The U.S. Embassy flag at half-staff in Tel Aviv following the death of President John F. Kennedy

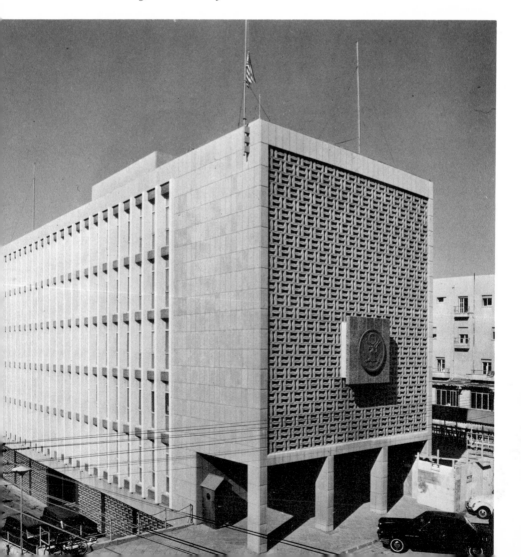

choose to retire there (this in itself puts an appreciable amount of money into the economy of the country), and with Israeli bonds bought in the United States or elsewhere which are freely cashable in Israel for use in that country. South African Jewry contributes more than that of any other single nation, and the communities of Montreal and Toronto probably give more per capita than any other groups. The greatest single sum contributed each year to the development of Israel is consistently that of the United Jewish Appeal which in the United States manages to sell enough bonds, to raise enough money to meet an annual target of one hundred to one hundred and thirty-five million dollars—by far the most successful fund-raising effort of any American charitable organization. This is the money that goes to bring water to the desert, to find a new home, a new job, a new life for refugees come from the four corners of the earth, most of them armed with little more than faith and hope. For the Jews of the United States and Canada and other countries, this is an opportunity to help their kinsmen re-establish the State of Israel in the land of their common origin. It is a source of pride to Jews everywhere, and certainly the existence of a proud and independent Jewish state within the community of nations has, within a decade and a half, created a new, international respect for the Jews, a strong, vigorous people with a place in the sun, and with their own articulate spokesmen—rather than the harried wanderers over the face of the earth, at the mercy of any despotic government in need of a scapegoat.

For Jews in America and Canada, pride in Israel and a helping hand is not incompatible with allegiance to their own governments. Their concern for Israel has its own special quality, but has much in common with Irish Americans marching down Fifth Avenue on St. Patrick's Day. It is important to remember the difference between the lot of the Jewish citizens of Canada, Britain, the United States and a very few other countries, and the survivors of the holocaust in Central and Eastern Europe. Israel is the answer for a great part of the Jewish world who can manage to make their way there.

Private American investment in Israel is sizeable. There are the familiar names of the Studebaker Lark and Helena Rubinstein's cosmetics, of the Sheraton and Hilton hotels, of many other things American. American investment can be expected to grow at an even faster tempo.

Israel's efforts to create a national economy which can stand on its own run from attracting tourists and foreign investment to unlikely exports and enterprises such as "Holyland Melons" and kosher wine, to a profitable merchant marine which in turn has created another merchant marine, the Black Star Line, for Ghana. A good part of the purchase of Israeli products and the use of Israeli services comes from Jews overseas. That part of Kennedy International Airport outside New York shared by the Israel line El Al and the Irish national airline is known as the Sentimental Corner.

Israeli emphasis on Afro-Asian and Latin American aid is a key to the future when Israel hopes to be able to apply most of her energies to making a better life for the hundreds of thousands of new citizens, to making the desert bloom again, to sharing with its neighbors new techniques for restoring all that land that was once known as the Fertile Crescent. Each new African state which accepts aid from Israel—and most of them are sensitive, wary, and proudly independent—is then just that much more likely to resist pressures from the Arab world to censure Israel, and, instead, to support motions in the United Nations and elsewhere calling on both the Arab states and Israel to resolve their differences.

At the same time it works toward a tolerant and peaceful future, the government of Israel is determined that none of us today shall forget the slaughter and the savagery of the recent

Students from Guinea receive instruction in fruit cultivation

past. To those of us who did not experience it personally, it seems a part of a nightmare and not really credible that a highly educated state in our own times should have set out to exterminate a group of people of whom it disapproved, many of them its own citizens. The idea is so terrible that the involuntary response of almost anyone is to avoid too close an examination of what happened, and to concentrate on one's own problems. Yet what the Nazi regime attempted differed only in degree—a horrifying degree—to what others have tried to do to other groups of men throughout history. What David Ben-Gurion of Israel planned in the trial of Adolph Eichmann was not only to make a single man accountable for his acts, which he was, and fairly by the standards of international law, but to provide a warning of what man can do to man. Speaking as just one observer, I can say only that I agree with friends, formerly officers in the British government of Palestine, who said that at first they feared the Eichmann trial would serve only to open old wounds, further to fire existing hatreds. But, bit by bit, as the evidence of what really happened was driven home again and again, they came to believe that it was best to face the terrible truth of prejudice and all that it cloaks, rather than let it simmer below the surface, ready to erupt again.

Israel's course now is to face this perilous past, and to build on the future. It is only a little more than a decade since Israel accepted an American government technical assistance program: everything from roads and help in bringing water to the Negev to training cowboys and, above all, sending many American experts to work in Israel and even more Israelis to study in the United States. Now Israel has agreed that it is time for the American overseas aid people to move on to countries in greater need (though need in Israel does still exist), and is itself sending surgeons and specialists in irrigation, construction engineers and poultrymen, experts of all sorts to the new nations of Asia and Africa; and also to some of the older ones of the Latin Americas who still must solve a number of the same problems that Israel as a small, new, pioneering land with few resources has learned to tackle at home. In this export of brains and talent, as with the settling of the desert and the frontier regions, and the defense of Israel itself, the youth of the country plays a leading part. Brigadier General S. L. A. Marshall, while noting the "veteran steadiness and emotional maturity" of the Army of Israel, is most particularly struck by its youthful vigor, noting that officers are retired in their forties, and that the average age in all ranks is three to four years younger than in any other army.

Two new Israel citizens

A boy wearing the traditional coronet of leaves at the Shavuot, the Pentecost festival

An elderly Israeli reading the scriptures

What all this adds up to, I think, has been firmly yet tenderly expressed by an Israeli writer named Fay Doron in a short essay in *The Jerusalem Post*. She notes a malaise, a tone of complaint in the air, now that the first, fighting, pioneering days are over. "The miracle of Israel has become a commonplace, an everyday affair." She recalls the visit by Sholem Asch, the Polish-American novelist and dramatist, to a woman settler in the State of Israel in the tough early days. Speaking in Yiddish the settler said, "If you have a talent for Eretz Yisrael, living here isn't so difficult."

"Without that talent," comments Mrs. Doron, "the process seems too hard; with it, no difficulties seem completely insuperable. But it is not necessarily an innate talent. It can be cultivated and nurtured. For some people, it is enough to watch the changing play of light on the stones of Jerusalem, to look upon the tortured wastes of the Negev awaiting redemption, and hear in their hearts the voices of fearless children at play. Still others find what they want in the strident sound of jet fighters screaming across the sky in practice for our protection. Yet others may find it in the open and unself-conscious wearing of the prayer-fringes. Each one of us, if he has only the embryo of that talent for Israel, can find sustenance for its sturdy growth."

Fay Doron goes on: "Our ancestors murmured in revolt against being taken to the Promised Land. They yearned for the fleshpots of Egypt, and even made a golden calf while Moses communed with the Almighty on the peak of Sinai. But their children who entered the Land developed a talent for Eretz Yisrael so strong and so persistent that two million of us have returned to the ancestral home."

This, to me, is what it is all about. The Israelis have come home.

BIBLIOGRAPHY

Books

GROLLENBERG, L. H. *Atlas of the Bible*. Thomas Nelson & Sons, New York, 1957.

MIKES, GEORGE, with BENTLEY, NICHOLAS. *Milk and Honey*. British Book Centre, New York, 1951.

PARKES, JAMES WILLIAM. *A History of Palestine from 135 A.D. to Modern Times*. Oxford University Press, New York, 1949.

SAMUELS, GERTRUDE. *B-G Fighter of Goliaths: The Story of Ben-Gurion*. Thomas Y. Crowell Company, New York, 1961.

WILSON, EDMUND. *The Scrolls from the Dead Sea*. Oxford University Press, New York, 1955.

Pamphlets

Facts About Israel (Available in Israeli Consulates and Government Tourist Offices in the United States.) Ministry of Foreign Affairs, Information Division, Jerusalem, Israel.

Israel Government Year Book. Government Printing Press, Jerusalem, Israel.

GLOSSARY

GLOSSARY

Aramaic   the vernacular of the country at the time of Christ.

Ashkenazim   the Jews of northern and eastern Europe.

Bedouin   a nomadic Arab.

Diaspora   the exile of those Jews scattered across the world following the capture of Jerusalem by the Roman Emperor Titus in 70 A.D.

Eretz Israel   Hebrew, meaning "land of Israel."

Fedayin   Arab guerilla raiders making forays into Israel.

Gadna   the Israeli Youth Corps for boys and girls from fourteen to eighteen.

Habimah   the Israel National Theater.

Hadassah   the Women's Zionist Organization of America founded in 1912 to support medical and nursing work in Israel.

Haganah   secret organization for Jewish self-defense in Palestine, now part of Israel Defense Forces.

Hamsin   Arabic for the sharaf, the hot wind from the southern Arabian desert.

Hannukah   an 8-day feast in the fall of each year which commemorates the victory of Judah the Maccabee over Antiochus Epiphanes in 165 B.C. and the subsequent rededication of the Temple. After the destruction of the Temple the festival was linked with the miracle of the cruse of oil which burned for eight days and the ceremony of kindling lights was instituted.

Hora	the national dance of Israel, a folk dance originally from the Balkans.
Kibbutzim	rural settlements in which all land, equipment and buildings are jointly owned and which provide communal care of children.
Knesset	the national legislature of Israel.
Kol Israel	the Israeli national radio.
Koran	the holy book of the Moslems.
Kosher	sanctioned by Jewish law, especially food which may be eaten as ritually clean.
Ladino	Judeo-Spanish based on medieval Castilian, spoken by the descendants of the Sephardim, expelled from Spain in 1492 and from Portugal in 1496.
Ma'abarot	transient camps for immigrants to Israel.
Maccabiah	the quadrennial Jewish games, named for the Maccabees who ruled the last independent kingdom of Israel.
Menorah	the traditional branched candelabrum used on Hannukah and other feasts.
Moshavim	smallholders' rural settlements with private ownership of property, but cooperative marketing and equipment.
Nahal	abbreviation for "Fighting Pioneer Youth," a branch of the Israel Defense Forces which trains volunteers for service in frontier agricultural settlements.
Palmach	the commando force of the Haganah.
Payot	traditional earlocks worn by certain ultra-Orthodox Jews.

Rabbi	"master," the religious leader who provides spiritual guidance to co-religionists in his community.
Rabbinate	the central rabbinical authority of Israel, located in Jerusalem.
Sabra	"Cactus"; a native-born Israeli.
Salaam	an Arabic salutation, the equivalent of the Hebrew "Shalom."
Shalom Aleichem	the usual Hebrew greeting, meaning "peace unto you," generally abbreviated in Israel to "Shalom."
Sephardim	descendants of the Spanish and Portuguese Jews.
Sharaf	Hebrew for the hot wind from the southern Arabian desert which blows each spring and fall.
Shofar	the ram's horn, blown on Jewish High Holy Days.
Yeshivot	the colleges which have taught and interpreted the Hebrew Holy Scriptures, both civil and spiritual, through the centuries.
Yeshu	Hebrew for Jesus.
Yiddish	a language derived from Middle High German, with strong Hebrew and Slavic influences.
Yom Kippur	the Day of Atonement.

Index

Italicized numbers refer to photographs.

ABOUT THE AUTHOR

Oden Meeker has written several well-known books, among them REPORT ON AFRICA which received an Anisfield-Wolf award and a citation from the National Council of Christians and Jews. This is his first book written specifically for young adults although THE LITTLE WORLD OF LAOS has been highly recommended by Young Adult reviewers.

Now Chief of CARE in Costa Rica, Mr. Meeker previously served in that capacity in Israel, India, Laos, and Hong Kong. An experienced traveler, he has been in more than 125 countries.

Mr. Meeker is the author of many magazine articles which have appeared in *The New Yorker, The Reporter, Harpers,* and others.

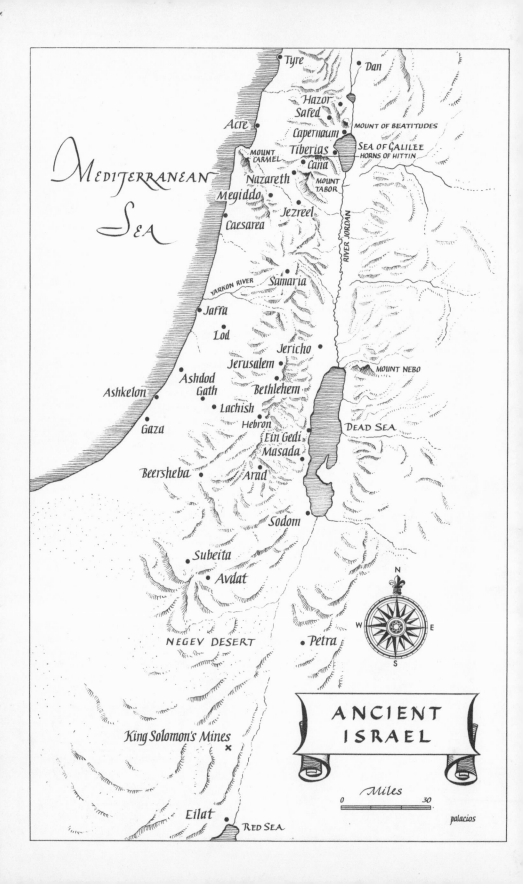

Tyre

Dan

Hazor
Safed

MOUNT OF BEATITUDES

Acre

Capernaum

MOUNT
CARMEL

Tiberias

SEA OF GALILEE
HORNS OF HITTIN

Cana

Nazareth

MOUNT TABOR

Megiddo

Jezreel

Caesarea

MEDITERRANEAN

SEA

RIVER JORDAN

YARKON RIVER

Samaria

Jaffa

Lod

Jericho

MOUNT NEBO

Jerusalem

Ashdod
Gath

Bethlehem

Ashkelon

Lachish

Gaza

Hebron

Ein Gedi

DEAD SEA

Masada

Beersheba

Arad

Sodom

Subeita

Avdat

N

W   E

S

NEGEV DESERT

Petra

ANCIENT
ISRAEL

King Solomon's Mines
✗

Miles

0   30

Eilat

RED SEA

palacios